W9-DDX-706

Raising
Resilience

ALSO BY TOVAH P. KLEIN

How Toddlers Thrive

Raising
Resilience

How to Help Our Children
THRIVE in Times of Uncertainty

Tovah P. Klein, PhD
with Billie Fitzpatrick

Foreword by Amy Schumer

HARPER

An Imprint of HarperCollins*Publishers*

FIRST EDITION

Designed by Kyle O'Brien

Library of Congress Cataloging-in-Publication Data

Names: Klein, Tovah P., author. | Fitzpatrick, Billie, other.
Title: Raising resilience : how to help our children thrive in times of uncertainty / Tovah P. Klein ; with Billie Fitzpatrick ; foreword by Amy Schumer.
Identifiers: LCCN 2024019069 (print) | LCCN 2024019070 (ebook) | ISBN 9780063286566 (hardcover) | ISBN 9780063286580 (ebook)
Subjects: LCSH: Resilience (Personality trait) in children. | Child development.
Classification: LCC BF723.R46 K57 2024 (print) | LCC BF723.R46 (ebook) | DDC 155.4/124—dc23/eng/20240509
LC record available at https://lccn.loc.gov/2024019069
LC ebook record available at https://lccn.loc.gov/2024019070

24 25 26 27 28 LBC 5 4 3 2 1

To my parents, Robert and Nancy. I am who I am because of you

To Kenny. Who walks alongside me

Contents

Foreword by Amy Schumer

Our son, Gene, was born on a rainy Sunday in May. We brought him home, put him in his crib in his thoughtfully decorated, pink room (because I promised myself not to conform to gender roles), and let out a long exhale. Not wanting to leave his side, I immediately sat in the gliding chair I had ordered and began to rock as I fed him. Looking down at his tiny head, I took a deep breath and realized that I had done it. All the agony I had endured in my pregnancy—the endless vomiting, the dehydration (I had hyper- emesis gravidarum), and the anxious waiting—was now, finally, be- hind me. Or was it? Parenting is nothing if not one foot in front of the other, a daily battle with one's fear of something happening to this most precious being and an absolute compulsion to protect them at all costs.

So when my husband, Chris, and I gave our son his first sponge bath and wound up soaking wet, head to toe, we laughed in relief and exhaustion and faced a searing question: Were we really up to this gigantic task of parenting? And when did that word become a verb, anyway? But like so many parents before us, we were in it . . . for good.

As the days and night passed, the lack of sleep driving Chris and me both a little bat-shit crazy, I turned to something that I have learned doing stand-up: my belief that getting up on stage always presents the possibility of failing, which sadly is the only way to get stronger and better.

Two years later, with COVID upon us, threatening us inside and out, Chris and I marched up to the Barnard Toddler Center and met Tovah Klein, the director extraordinaire. Good friends had sung Tovah's praises, and like many other ambitious parents on the Upper West Side, we wanted in. More to the point, we wanted our darling son to become part of an exceptional early childhood program where he would learn not only some early school skills but also, and perhaps more importantly, the social and emotional competencies for being a loving, empathetic, and decent human being.

With Chris and me both clutching Gene's tiny hands, Tovah Klein smiled and said, confidently and calmly, "Hello!" Something about her eye contact and her manner let us know we were *all* going to be okay. And, just like that, and in spite of COVID raging, Gene was thriving at the Toddler Center: He learned to have fun, fumble, and fail. He learned to be part of a group, partner up, and listen to his own inner drummer. He played with blocks and logs; he sang out of tune; and over the next two years, we watched our little boy become a marvelous if imperfect being. Tovah said this was all about helping children become resilient.

Tovah became our fearless guide through the next year and still is to this day. Her love for children and deep knowledge of what children need to thrive is apparent in all she does and how she interacts with children. Yes, she guides young children as they build resilience from their very earliest days. But, in addition, Tovah teaches us parents, too. Her patience and empathy helped us get through the fear-wracking hell that living through COVID entailed. Tovah helped us separate from our son so he could be his own person, knowing we were nearby. She also taught us how to believe in ourselves, trust our instincts, and learn to support our child—not with rules, formulas, or checklists but by helping us discover what we know best: how to love our child in a way that enables him to grow and thrive.

Our baby boy is on his way to kindergarten, and when it comes time to let go of his now-bigger hands next September, we, his parents, may be bubbling with nerves, but I know he will be ready to roll.

Let Tovah be your guide as she's been ours and thousands of parents' before. I thought the Toddler Center was a school for two-year-olds, but I learned it was a school for us parents. Her researched knowledge and attention armed us to be the kind of confident leaders we needed to be for our son and for ourselves. She is a gift to us and future generations of leaders and, more importantly, is good people. I am so thrilled we, as parents, get to read this book. Her first, *How Toddlers Thrive*, served as gospel in our house. And the result is a happy, independent, empathetic child who knows how to socialize and be a loved member of a community, and parents who do the same. I will never stop being grateful to you, Tovah, and to Jess Seinfeld, for recommending we bring our son and ourselves into your world. Thank you, friend.

Amy Schumer

Raising
Resilience

Introduction

I've been thinking about the themes of this book for a long time, but only began writing about them as the world shut down in response to a global pandemic. My subject—raising children who can handle, get through, and thrive during and after times of uncertainty—soon became more pressing and immediate. The pandemic provided a one-of-a-kind living laboratory where I could simultaneously observe and experience my approach to parenting in an extended experiment as I watched parents and children encounter circumstances that often made them feel powerless and vulnerable. My family and I, living in New York City, were participants in this unfolding experiment as well.

While the pandemic-induced lockdown was a situation new to nearly all of us, aspects of it were also familiar to me and the work that I do. As a child psychologist, I've specialized in the effects of traumatic situations on children and families, investigating the impact of abuse, homelessness, natural disasters, and tragic events such as 9/11. I knew from my previous and ongoing research that children and adults had the capacity to emerge changed but not scarred from tragedy—if certain factors were in place. Specifically, when parents stay connected and attuned and provide children with emotional safety and security, they create a protective effect against lasting harm, even in the toughest situations.

My earlier work pointed to this protective potential, but as we all began to resettle into life postpandemic, I wanted to look deeper into what parents were doing so effectively to create such long-lasting, positive outcomes for their children. It had to do with helping their children become resilient, but how? What else was happening within the parent-child relationship that was not only protective but also fortifying?

Answering these questions has resulted in this book, which offers parents a strategic approach to helping their children become resilient now and into the future. Resilience is not simply an ability to bounce back after disappointments or loss; it's not just the ability to adapt to changes big and small. In my thirty-plus years of working with children and their parents, as well as conducting original research and population-wide studies, I have come to understand resilience with more nuance and see it as a set of characteristics that parents can teach their children, nurturing it through their everyday interactions. Often, when we use the term "resilience," we assume that we become resilient as simply a result of making it through a difficult time, facing adversities or surviving a trauma or some other challenging event. And while overcoming hardship can strengthen a person and *show* their resilience, it does not have to take hardship or tragedy to *build* resilience.

As we all emerged from our pandemic haze, I theorized two core facets of resilience: one, that the parent-child relationship itself was some kind of resilience incubator that enabled children to develop the inner resources to adapt and adjust well; and two, that through this relationship, parents could help children build resilience proactively before the arrival of a crisis or traumatic experience. Exciting recent neurobiological research into trauma supports this view: the presence of a connected, tuned-in, loving parent makes the difference between a child being negatively (and sometimes permanently) scarred by adverse experiences versus not; evidence also shows that the presence of a connected parent helps children lay down the foundation for self-regulation—which is the neurobiological system that enables us to regain balance and stability and bounce back from any degree or level of disruption.

In this way, I see this book as a reframe of what it means to be resilient—of how resilience develops and is shaped over time, and why it matters. When we accept that uncertainty is a given in life, not an aberration, then nurturing resilience becomes an everyday opportunity—and it happens most fruitfully within the context of your relationship with your child. Resilience is an outcome of the care parents provide every single day, coupled with the kindness, attention, and reactions they show in response to what their child needs, whether that is comforting a child, picking them up at school, preparing dinner, or listening to them vent about their day. These interactions matter and add up to a relationship that becomes the incubator for resilience. This is not about perfection. It is about establishing and carrying out a loving, stable, and connected day-to-day relationship, as I will show you throughout this book.

If you've read my first book, *How Toddlers Thrive*, you will no doubt recognize some of the consistencies in what young and older children need to grow and develop optimally. This time I am addressing parents of children of all ages, identifying and expanding upon the universals of what grounds children and teens and helps them form a strong base to grow into thriving human beings. (Throughout this book I use the term "parent" to refer to all caregivers, including guardians and others who have formative relationships with children.)

In my primary role as director of Barnard College's Center for Toddler Development and in related work with parents of older children and teens, I have the pleasure of wearing many hats (sometimes many at once!) on any given day—that of educator, clinician, researcher, and advocate, from teaching college students, parents, and professionals about child development and the many individual ways children vary, to conducting research aimed at understanding parental impacts on children, to interpreting these studies to advocate for children's needs, to working directly with parents and children. I spend my days asking what children and teens need to establish a foundation for healthy, adaptable, compassionate growth no matter what life throws their way. It's one thing to learn how to address a challenging behavior that your four- or fourteen-year-old zings you with so you have a way to handle it the next time. It's another matter altogether to understand what motivates such behaviors so you can learn how to relate better to your child and solve these issues for the long run and in a way that helps them, too. In other words, I will show you ways to support your child's optimal development so they learn to become resilient now and into the future.

Over the last several decades, many important studies connecting developmental psychology to neurobiology have been conducted. I see my role as translating this valuable body of work, along with my own research on parents and children, and offering families an approach that asks you to make a slight perspective shift and think about parenting in the context of your relationship with your child. Instead of parenting from a top-down perspective, you create a relationship with your child that acts as both container and anchor. As the anchor, parents function like a stable moor that steadies the so-called boat that is the growing child, keeping it from being tossed about in strong currents or storms. When a child can rely on this steadying force, they are more likely to internalize a sense of safety along with the knowledge that they will be okay, despite a storm or change in their midst. As the anchor, you help steady your child emotionally and physically when they are unsure or upset and give them the tools to become their independent, confident, and compassionate selves.

As containers, parents build and nurture a relationship that offers children a physical and emotional space where they can experience and express all of their feelings. The containing relationship enables a child to learn how to manage intense, negative feelings because the child comes to know they are not alone. By providing this safe space, children are encouraged to be their authentic self, without ridicule, judgment, or shame. Every child needs a place where they are accepted fully and understood, and the parent relationship that acts as a container provides this sense of security.

You may not necessarily be aware of how you are already acting as an anchor and container, but it is what you do when you calm your upset child or handle a meltdown, set a reasonable limit regarding jumping on the couch or cell phone use, set up a routine for bedtime or to do homework, or help them handle their worries about starting high school. The challenge, of course, is that the work of anchoring and containing (being in a relationship is work after all) isn't always easy to do in the context of real life. You may have moments when it feels nearly impossible, when emotions run high for you and for your child or teen, or when you feel like you have not a single ounce of patience left. At times like these, it will be harder to hold and anchor them—and yourself, for that matter.

I've been there, too, as a mother myself. My approach is not about perfection, it's about practicality. I've developed five pillars that give shape to the developmental and neurobiological underpinnings of resilience and show you concrete ways to be both a container and an anchor whether your child is two, ten, or sixteen. I provide many time-tested strategies for busy, stressed-out parents, and for parents who are feeling okay and just want to do a better job at helping their child become more adaptable. The strategies are not autocratic codes of behavior. Rather these are clearly defined guideposts you can depend on to help your children learn foundational skills to grow and develop emotionally, intellectually, and socially—regardless of their personality, temperament, background, or experiences of stressors or trauma. They are applicable to every child at every age. When parents are able to step in and provide reliable, loving stability to their children, great things can happen. And that's perhaps a bonus: when you use this approach and incorporate the five pillars, you nurture a lifelong relationship with your child, one that both of you will value for years to come.

My approach supports parents as well as children. You will discover insightful examples from the field that offer you a source of succor and support, as well as a series of Reflective Questions to prompt connections between your past experience and your parenting now. Clearly, during times of uncertainty, everyone has to work a little harder to stay grounded and focused on what matters most—the well-being of our children. Feeling unstable, as we do when life's uncertainty increases, can interfere with our best intentions, making us more anxious and worried. This is why becoming aware of our responses as parents helps us manage our *own* emotions and worries first, without unwittingly hoisting them onto our children. Often, at times of accelerated emotions, we move fast, too fast, without giving ourselves the time to figure out the best route. We act out of our own fears and our unwavering desire to protect our children. We can act without thinking. When this happens, we run the risk of stepping in too forcefully, even when it is in a loving way. We can undermine our children's natural ability to grow a sense of agency and ability to overcome challenges, which they need as a foundation for positive growth. Beyond this, parents' well-intended yet overly forward actions can sometimes shame their children rather than support their growth. My approach guides parents to find the sweet spot where they are present and grounded themselves and thereby able to offer guidance and, when appropriate, let go so children can safely test their own resilience.

The book is organized in two parts. Part one, "The Roots of Resilience," establishes the foundation of my approach by first acknowledging why times of uncertainty feel so disruptive and anxiety-provoking to all of us, parents and children alike. Then we'll examine what we can learn from dealing with stress, adversity, and traumatic experiences and why it is important to understand this in order to help children grow on a daily basis, establishing the foundations they need to face life whether times are smooth or rough. Part one also includes an explanation of the psychology and neurobiology of the attachment relationship, the core of how you first connect to your child and how you can continue to build this connection as your child becomes more independent. This relationship is directly tied to how children cope in life, handle emotions and the obstacles they will inevitably face, all on the road to building resilience. You'll learn to see, as well, the influence your own childhood experience brings to your parenting, a key factor in understanding your relationship with your child, your reactions to them, and how to best support them. This process involves looking at how you were raised, including identifying the missing pieces or missed opportunities in your up-bringing that may be silently driving your anxiety and actions with your children.

Part two focuses on the five pillars of your child's resilience, pre-sented alongside numerous practical strategies that parents can use in the here and now to help their child build the capacities that un-dergird resilience. The five pillars show parents how to:

1. Provide emotional safety so your child can build inner trust
2. Help your child learn how to emotionally regulate so they can manage their emotions
3. Establish limits alongside freedom to make mistakes, so that your child feels motivated to explore and learn
4. Connect with your child, so they develop social skills, empathy, and the confidence to connect authentically with others
5. Accept your child for who they are, without judgment or shame, so they accept and love themselves, the key to well-being, happiness, and compassion

These pillars of resilience are not a linear set of guidelines but can be used in whatever manner or order makes most sense to you and your family. Together they will enable your child to thrive, even through the toughest times. At the end of the day, when it can often feel like raising children today gets to be daunting, I return to the fact that I am an incurable optimist, filled with hope for our futures. My optimism stems from the fact that I've seen hundreds—if not thousands—of children and parents pull through countless situations that at first looked insurmountable, and with support and connection watched them move forward with strength and resilience. In every child, adolescent, and emerging adult is a young person poised to grow, learn, and flourish despite inevitable imperfections of their environment or obstacles in their path. I view parents in a similar light: as individuals who come to parenting with their own history and who want above all to do what's best for their child, even when it is hard. In all of our lives, disappointments, fears, loss, and pain are inevitable, but they also provide opportunities for parents to help their children to adapt and grow. These challenging moments are the unintended gifts of building resilience.

Raising children is not only for today, or this moment; it is a lifelong endeavor. The benefits of nurturing your relationship with your child, with eyes simultaneously on the present and the future, give children a robust, ongoing opportunity to build the emotional and social skills that will enable them to become their full selves— independent, resourceful people who are caring and compassionate toward others and, importantly, able to handle the ups and downs of life and thrive. And just as important is raising children who want to return home to you even when they are grown-up and out in the world.

PART I

The Roots of Resilience

CHAPTER 1

The Opportunity During Times of Uncertainty

Global pandemic, high death rates, racial and social unrest, a fragile economy, social isolation, and climate disasters. Any one of these factors can create a sense of uncertainty. And of course, during times of uncertainty, it's natural to feel more anxious, especially as a parent caring and responsible for children. You begin to doubt your own instincts, feel less assured about how to engage with your children, and go into generalized worry mode, imagining long-range consequences as foregone conclusions. From this vantage point, many parents look toward the future as if it's a vast and terrible unknown that is impossible to prepare for.

These concerns are not unreasonable. As a child psychologist specializing in the effects of population-wide trauma, I have made it my life's work to understand how to best set up children to thrive in spite of adversity. Even before the pandemic, large-scale social changes were impacting everyday family life. The ubiquitous presence of and near-total reliance on technology, the pernicious influence of social media, the dwindling opportunities for in-person anything, and the growing dread related to climate change have been threatening the health and well-being of children and teens—all of it placing an increasing pressure on parents to protect children from a future that is hard to imagine. Without a doubt, parents today feel overwhelmed and often insecure, unable to trust that they know how best to raise our children under so much stress—both concrete and existential.

Even in the best of times, being a parent requires hard and intentional work. The responsibility to protect, nurture, and take care of our most precious beings challenges us at our core—regardless of our resources—and can make us feel exquisitely vulnerable. During times of uncertainty this vulnerability is heightened further. Even everyday changes can make us feel less grounded. In this state, any event that creates upheaval in our day-to-day lives has the potential to set off a threat response at the cellular level of our brains and bodies. When activated, this automatic fight-flight-freeze response increases our anxiety and makes it difficult to discern between real harm and imagined dangers. Our reactions and the way our brains respond to both seemingly small incidents of change and bigger, even traumatic, events follow similar neurobiological patterns because as humans we rely on the same pathways of responding to stress regardless of the magnitude of the stressor. (You'll read more about this innate human stress response in chapter four.)

In such a heightened state of alarm and worry, it becomes difficult to not only stay grounded and clear on how best to raise our children but also remember a remarkable, hope-filled truth: that given the neuroplasticity of our brains (the ability of the brain to change or rewire based on new experiences), we all have the capacity to adapt to even the harshest challenges. This ability to adapt is essential to our survival and key to building resilience and bouncing back after hardship and trauma. Think of a stroke patient who is unable to move their hand initially, but gradually and with practice regains this ability as the brain adapts and restores function. Or how a young student with ADHD learns to focus and gains confidence once his parents move him to a more supportive middle school. A child I worked with following the World Trade Center attacks reacted with hour-long tantrums and sleep refusals if an alarm went off in the apartment building to which they fled when the planes hit the nearby towers, or if he heard any sirens. With support from his parents and practice with an alarm that he could turn on and off himself, the tantrums lessened, and he stopped having such strong reactions. His brain readapted to this noise and learned that it was no longer a threat. So while the stress of uncertainty tests our capacity to adapt, it's hugely important to our ability to learn and incorporate new information, use knowledge and emotional understanding to adjust to new environments, and face and move through hard situations and establish our equilibrium again—all of which comprise the essence of resilience.

During the pandemic, I conducted a research study of over one hundred families of children under the age of eight to develop a more nuanced understanding of the psychological and social impact brought on by the uncertainty accompanying the large-scale effects of the pandemic. I wanted to understand how parents and children responded, then adapted to the unprecedented situation. The number one reported behavioral change in children during the first year of the pandemic was regression—reverting to bed-wetting, night awakenings, or using baby talk, and an inability to take care of themselves in ways they did in the past. For older children this meant a greater reliance on parents and some loss of independence. I spoke with one parent whose preschooler—typically a happy, healthy eater—refused to eat anything for a number of days in response to the rapid changes and stress at home. (With the intervention of their pediatrician, she got back on track.) Sibling rivalries often became more intense in children of all ages, causing fights that further escalated the stress quotient of the home environment. From a psychological point of view, these behavioral changes showed children in the midst of adjusting to new circumstances. Was it the pandemic itself or the sudden need to adjust wrought by the pandemic that caused such reactions? My research and experience point to the latter.

Let me explain.

Any kind of change requires readjustment—emotionally, physically, cognitively. Major life changes ask us to interact with our peers or families in slightly (or greatly) different ways. Sometimes these adjustments happen automatically. Sometimes it can take longer—a day, week, even a year—but gradually we get the hang of the new route to town or find a new favorite supermarket or playground. These adjustments may seem inconsequential, even superficial. But let's say you're an older person for whom it takes more energy and time to drive to the supermarket; for that person, learning a new route can feel inordinately stressful, even upsetting. Or say you've been sick with the flu, and when you arrive at your regular dry cleaner to find it closed because of new hours, you just lose it and start to cry. We've all had those days when one little exception to the rule feels like just too much. Internally, we are trying hard to assert the so-called status quo by sticking to the familiar—in spite of the new and changed circumstances. This is why we like routines: they ground and comfort us. The familiar brings a feeling of calm to our minds and nervous systems. When we encounter change, our brains are more or less hardwired to go through a sequence of adjustments. First, we become aware of the change; next, we try to determine if we can handle the change (an assessment that can cause varying degrees of anxiety or excitement); and then we react—either adjusting well or adjusting with difficulty . . . or somewhere in between the two. Neither is right or wrong.

People who are able to adjust with more ease can be considered flexible or more adaptable; those who have a tougher time making adjustments might be referred to as more rigid. These are not value judgments but rather speak to a very real and partially inborn continuum of adaptability. Most people are readily adaptable some of the time, and less so at other times; adaptability and rigidity can vary depending on the circumstances. The good news is that we can all learn to become more adaptable and adjust to change with greater ease, which means becoming more resilient. This, again, points to the nature of neuroplasticity.

At its root, adapting under pressure is about resilience, which is neither a trait nor a static ability that we either possess or don't possess. Resilience and the capacity to adjust optimally rely on a set of inner resources that can be developed and honed. These resources form the five pillars that I will further describe in the chapters of part two:

1. The trust that you'll be okay despite a present stressor
2. An ability to manage your emotions
3. The motivation to act or assert some control over a situation
4. The awareness to ask for help and connect with others
5. A belief that you matter

These resources are built over time and in response to events and experiences of our lives. However, the parent-child relationship provides a unique opportunity to help our children develop these resources of resilience. Each time we help a child through a challenge, small or large, and help them become more self-aware, they become better able to manage tough emotions that might otherwise interfere with daily functioning—like getting on the school bus, socializing with peers, playing a new sport, or taking a test. When we are there, on the sidelines, as they develop agency and learn that it's okay to ask for help, they build the internal knowledge that they can handle present and future challenges. And when we stay connected and attuned, letting them know they are valued, loved, and accepted for who they are, children develop a strong center, like a reservoir from which they draw when encountering stress and difficulties.

These core resources of resilience are crucial to our children's ability to live full, meaningful lives. They enable them to pivot and move on; to engage and learn now and always; to not only survive severe situations but also thrive despite the pain and loss that can accompany trauma. There will always be stress and challenges in your child's life; that piece is certain. And none of this is meant to overlook or oversimplify the significant hardships and tragedies that many families experience; there is no doubt that trauma, particularly when compounded by multiple traumas, can leave people with long-lasting scars, and resources and support are needed to help alleviate such outcomes. Yet, within and outside of these perilous situations, parents are situated to respond in ways that both buffer the impact and support the growth of their children. If we can support our children to benefit from positive responses during times of stress, we are setting them up to succeed in life.

The Protective Effects of the Parent Relationship

My interest in the parent-child relationship began early and challenged me almost immediately. One of my first opportunities to learn about this dynamic was when, as a teenager, I worked in a summer program for children with a range of emotional and social challenges. One child, Emma, stuck out to me and still does to this day. She was four years old and abused by a mother with severe mental illness whose parental rights were being terminated.

Anytime a limit was set for Emma by a teacher (it's not okay to hit other children, for example), she screamed loudly and nearly uncontrollably for her mother. Initially, I was stunned by this behavior, but I soon became intrigued by the power of this person, the only caregiver she knew. In times when little Emma felt frustrated or vulnerable, she called for the person who'd hurt her and made her feel unsafe, still hoping for protection. This observation made me curious about the powerful role of parents and children's core needs to feel safe and seek protection—so core that they would even call for an abusive parent during a time of need. I did not yet know terms like "toxic stress," "trauma," "attachment," or "resilience," but soon I would begin to learn about them and view them as related. What could happen when bad and hurtful things befell children, and what could parents do to ensure that children did not suffer long-term negative impacts? What essential role did parents play in how their children developed, especially when facing negative or potentially harmful events in their lives? These questions have motivated me for decades.

Later, while an undergraduate student at the University of Michigan, I chose to study and further investigate the underpinnings of parent-child attachment relationships. These were the early days of attachment studies. I filmed dozens of parent-child attachment protocols, called Strange Situations, the now-well-known research paradigm to assess the factors that defined the quality of the parent-child attachment relationship. Samuel Meisels, my mentor, was studying how early attachment could impact a child's socialization abilities in preschool in a sample of children born prematurely. With my young and not-yet-trained eyes, I observed a wide range of how children reacted when their parents left the room as part of the protocol and then returned. Some children shut down, some screamed, some played. At reunion, most babies, regardless of the intensity of their behavior in response to their mother leaving, felt comforted, settled down, and fairly quickly returned to their exploration and playing. In other words, trust and curiosity returned to the child once their main caregiver, their security, came back. But I was concerned and curious about these children who were unable or reticent to play or engage again in their environment when the parent returned.

This smaller number of children shut down and sat still; they cried and could not be consoled; or they moved away from the mother and turned their back to her. What was it about the qualities of the relationship that was so necessary for a child to thrive? I then began to wonder about the repercussions if bad things occurred within that dyad—the relationship between parent and child. Could negative impacts be overcome? And if so, how, and what would that look like? I left college with many burning questions about children and how to support them, but mostly with a desire to know more about these incredibly curious and developing people.

Next, I sought out an opportunity to work closely with children and families in the horrendous homeless shelter system in NYC in the late 1980s to closely examine the complexities affecting the parent-child relationship. I was able to work directly with young children, something I loved to do, and observe what happened to children when families were living in crowded conditions under extreme stress, facing a level of uncertainty and fear no one should ever have to deal with. Simultaneously and related to this hands-on work, I conducted research with a policy researcher, Janice Molnar at Bank Street College of Education, on children living in these homeless shelters (called "welfare hotels" at the time). It was disturbing to witness the level of stress and even terror families faced from the complex insults that would undermine any parent's ability to provide basic safety—from lack of permanent housing to violence to food insufficiency. And yet, what I also saw were mothers (most shelters only allowed mothers with children) who, against the odds, continued to find ways to protect their children from lasting harm. I also saw parents who, under the unbearable severe weight of it all, were unable to give their children the psychological or physical safety they needed. I asked myself, yet again, why can a subset of parents provide protective care even with unimaginable obstacles in their way while others, quite understandably given the circumstances, are unable to meet these essential needs of their children?

I knew from the research on attachment that in the early years of childhood it's not necessarily the outward circumstances or environment that define or establish the necessary sense of safety that children need to grow and develop optimally, although these can make establishing the needed security easier or more challenging. Instead, it is the *quality* of the interactions with their parents or guardians that matter most. What I was observing was exactly this phenomenon: as harsh and difficult as the situation was in a homeless shelter, a number of families with small children, now squeezed into a dark and cramped housing situation, were doing okay. I observed certain ways that parents connected and provided the necessary support despite the adverse circumstances:

- They were present and attuned to a child's physical *and* emotional needs
- They were calm and supportive in their interactions with their children, able to focus on calming them when upset or disoriented
- They encouraged their children to play and explore their environment; when able, they engaged in play and shared joy with their children
- They stayed connected amidst chaotic situations and set up routines for the day

My observations of families in the shelters were consistent with the research: parents, when aware and attuned, even when faced with the harsh realities of minimal financial or material resources or other major stressors, helped their children adapt, adjust, and grow. Parents could do so in spite of the stress on their brains and bodies that accompanies disturbing, disruptive, and entirely uncontrollable conditions. We titled this project *Home Is Where the Heart Is*, because it was clear to the research team that a sense of home and comfort was possible and necessary, no matter where one lived or the challenges they faced.

I witnessed this buffering effect taking place over and over again as I trained to be a psychologist and worked with children facing a range of serious life challenges—from physical and sexual abuse to parental loss to their own pediatric chronic or life-threatening illnesses, including pediatric AIDS. Often, the parents were struggling as well. And yet, what always mattered in terms of how well the child was doing was the quality of the relationship with their parent: the more solid the relationship, the more connected the parent, the better able the child was to adapt and adjust to the changing or stressful circumstances. Better adaptation meant greater building of resilience.

I was hopeful; if I could identify those protective factors, I might better understand how children get through stress and trauma and still develop on a healthy course forward. I also theorized that getting through these stressors could potentially make children stronger and more adaptable to any of life's future challenges. Not without costs, of course, but I was interested in the strengths-based focus and examined the protective roles parents exhibit under extreme conditions as key ingredients for attuned parenting and child development more generally.

It was this query that propelled me back to graduate school to better understand the nature of the relationship between parents and children. What enabled parents to be there for their children? I wondered. What did they need in terms of support to do this buffering work? Likewise, I was interested in knowing what could hinder them from being available and tuned in. I wanted to identify what parents do in their everyday interactions with children—from routines to loving care—that would take on elevated importance in times of trouble. I enrolled at Duke University to study developmental and clinical psychology under the guidance of Martha Putallaz, who was conducting groundbreaking research on the mutual influence of parents and peers on children's development, both optimal and problematic. I jumped into the work to look at memories and social frames parents bring from their childhood and use to socialize their children in the influential world of peer relations. I thought this line of research could help shed light on how some children succeed in the social world of peers and others flounder or are outright rejected, which puts them at risk for ongoing social, emotional, academic, and even physical problems.

My focus once again was to examine what processes could help or hurt a child in their development. The hopeful part of me thought about how to help parents who were struggling in this arena so their children would not have to follow in the same challenged pathway. You can call this the intersection of developmental and clinical psychology, where researchers focus on the continuum between optimal and potentially problematic development.

While conducting this parental influence research, I also began doing clinical work as part of my psychology doctoral training. Early on, I had the good fortune to meet Bessel van der Kolk, the author of *The Body Keeps the Score* and now considered one of the foremost experts on a neurobiological understanding of traumatic experience. At the time, van der Kolk was in the early stages of forming his theory that traumatic experiences were not only experienced and remembered in the brain but that the body's entire nervous system played an important role in how and why trauma has such a lasting effect on us. For many years, post-traumatic stress disorder (PTSD) was explained through the lens of soldiers having great difficulty reassimilating after wartime experience. His work widened trauma understanding to areas beyond war and helped to define how trauma settles deeply into the body and soul of a person. He was one of the first scientists to take the lid off of PTSD.

I shared his interest in the etiology and effects of trauma and was deeply impacted by a set of workshops he led. My research, however, focused more on understanding the world through the eyes of children. But I learned valuable insight into the nature of trauma from van der Kolk's work and his research with my clinical supervisor, Susan Roth, which helped frame my own questions. I knew that it's not solely the event itself that causes the trauma; there are multiple factors, which include a child's temperament and how they experience the events and their interpretation of it and the support they receive around it. So how could we—parents in particular—help shape the narrative that emerges about the event or situation? How does the buffering effect interfere so the trauma cannot take root in a child's brain-body system? How can parents help avoid creating behaviors around events that reinforce pain, shame, and suffering?

Why the Neurobiology of Attachment Matters

The protective effect that parents provide becomes wired into our cells and is rooted in the attachment relationship between parent and child. This initial relationship is not only an emotional bond but a neurobiologically supported system that enables infants and children to develop optimally. Infants are neurologically and physiologically wired to attach to caregivers and to motivate those caregivers to take care of their needs; similarly, the primary caregivers (usually parents) are more or less wired to stay close to children, attune to them, and respond to those basic needs. The seminal work of Columbia University researcher Myron Hofer zeroed in on this vital neurobiological connection between parent and child. Through his extensive research spanning decades, Hofer shows that the bond between parent and child acts as a "hidden" regulator for the child's nervous system. Understanding the mechanisms of how attachment initiates this regulating effect can help parents deepen their awareness of why they are so important to the optimal development of children's neural systems, the regulation of the child's brain-body, and their ability to manage stress and adapt to change.

The attachment relationship between parent and child is a powerful force that sets off a number of cascading biological, emotional, and cognitive processes. Over the past forty-plus years, the research into attachment has grown and deepened, revealing the underlying neurobiology of this relationship between parent/caregiver and child and how it fosters the development of a child's brain and nervous system. Specifically, a series of longitudinal studies conducted on Romanian orphans who were abandoned and placed in overcrowded institutions during years of dictatorship in the 1990s began to crack the code. At the same time, researchers at the University of Minnesota were following an at-risk group of infants through their childhood, along with their parents, to understand the role of attachment in ongoing development. These parallel studies described the vast impact of an early and ongoing attachment relationship as well as what happened when infants were deprived of this vital relationship.

Researchers followed the Romanian orphans from early infancy to adolescence and compared their development to that of Romanian children who had not experienced institutional care. The studies aimed to investigate the effects of parental separation/abandonment, severe deprivation, neglect, and institutional care on children's cognitive, emotional, and social development. The results were striking and revealed that children who had spent their early years in institutional care were at risk for significant developmental delays, including lower IQ scores, impaired language development, and emotional and behavioral problems. The studies also found that children who were adopted earlier in life, between six months and age two, and given access to a range of resources, had better outcomes than those who remained in institutional care longer; these results suggested that early intervention and subsequent secure attachment to a caregiver can help mitigate the negative effects of early deprivation. Given access to sensitive caregiving, early adopted children had the opportunity to adapt in positive ways.

While this research on deprivation is quite startling, it also provides crucial insights about what secure attachment does for a child's growing brain and nervous system and, as a result, how best to support and scaffold any child's development. It also points to the high cost of not having a consistent attachment figure. Like many studies that focus on problems or disease, the efforts helped clinicians, educators, and other researchers cue into both the fallout caused by early deprivation and the importance of the early attachment relationship and need for security.

Consider that newborns enter this world with what is estimated to be one hundred billion neurons. In order for their brains to make sense of all the signals from these neurons, they depend on the parent to help the development of the neural connections and regulate the signaling within the cells of the brain. Parents are like the chief organizers of a child's brain. Children require the parent's physical proximity and consistent care for the brain-body to form and function. The more responsive the caregiver or parent is, the more sound the neural connections and the more optimally the child develops—physically, emotionally, and cognitively—the very seeds of resilience.

There are many ways that parents help organize the baby's brain and body, beginning with meeting their essential needs—protection from danger, nutritious food, sufficient sleep, clothing and warmth, sensory stimulation, and sensitivity and attention. Once these basic needs are satisfied, parents build on this foundation through their daily interactions: nursing or feeding a baby, holding and snuggling, singing or talking with a baby or child, or attending to a child in distress. These parent behaviors may seem simple and quite natural—but you may recall from Hofer's research cited above, children are born already wired to *elicit* this behavior from parents. When a child cries, squeals, or smiles, they are signaling for their needs to be met—*I am hungry, I am uncomfortable, I need changing, I am happy and want to connect*. When a parent responds to these signals, they send powerful messages to the child's rapidly forming brain to make the necessary neural connections that provide the foundation for all areas of vital functioning, now and into the future.

More than a dozen major longitudinal studies (along with other short-term studies) also assessed attachment in the first year of life and mapped it onto development throughout childhood and adolescence, and even into adulthood. Across studies, researchers found that children who were securely attached early in life were better able to manage their emotions and showed fewer signs of anxiety as they got older. The attuned and connected parent reduces distress, blocks the release of stress hormones, and helps modulate emotions; the outcome is a potentially lifelong impact on the child's developing neurobiology. Secure attachment is further associated with greater cognitive skills (as measured by verbal reasoning, working memory, perceptual reasoning, and processing speed) and more sturdy immune systems. In sum, secure attachment is not the sole determining factor of optimal development, but it is a very vital one.

The quality of the parent-child relationship reflects the level of security and trust that the child derives from being in this primary attachment relationship. Early in the study of attachment, researchers Mary Ainsworth, Mary Blehar, Everett Waters, and Sally Wall identified three patterns of attachment quality by intensively studying the interactions between mothers and their infants over the first year of life. A fourth pattern was identified later. The main group of children identified were those who were classified as securely attached: infants whose parent was consistently present and attuned to them, enabling the infant to trust that the parent would respond to their needs and be available during times of distress; they showed distress and decreased play in a parents' absence and comfort and reengagement following the parents' return.

Two other distinct attachment styles were identified as insecure—ambivalent/resistant and avoidant—and as being patterns in infants who exhibited a lack of assuredness that the caregiver would be available to them in a time of need. Children who display avoidant attachment tend to avoid or ignore their caregiver upon return after leaving; they may turn their back or move away, even when in need—just like the children I observed as a college student who piqued my interest in studying the parent-child relationship. These avoidantly attached children tend not to seek comfort or support when distressed, giving them an appearance of early independence and of being self-reliant at a too-early age as they learn not to count on their parent to tune in to or respond to their needs. As a result, studies show they will develop a strategy of minimizing their emotional needs even when their stress hormones are high, an indicator of distress and a need for comfort. Instead, they tend to hold their emotions in. If a child feels no one will respond to their need, it is adaptive to minimize their feelings as a means of self-protection. Children with ambivalent/resistant attachment styles develop their own adaptive response to their caregiver's inconsistent pattern of responses—that is, sometimes responding sensitively and other times not, or overlooking or rejecting them. They tend to display clingy and overly dependent behaviors toward their caregivers as they show their lack of assuredness that the caregivers will be available to them and struggle to be comforted by the parents' return. Stemming from this lack of assuredness, they are hesitant to explore their environment, even with reassurance by an adult. Instead, they keep their focus on monitoring where the caregiver is.

While these identified attachment patterns, and decades of subsequent research, point to the essential need for a secure attachment, it's also important to keep in mind that attachment styles are not fully fixed. They can change over time. Relationships between a parent and child can adjust, often through supportive interventions.

Further, as children go out in the world there will be additional influences that impact their well-being, including forming bonds and relationships with other people who will stand in as attachment figures—family members, teachers, and other adults in their lives. This network of relationships points to the possibility of a "redo" for attachment, again hearkening back to the inherent plasticity of the human brain.

And yet, we also know that improving attachment relationships is a process that requires nuance to the child's needs and highly tuned-in care. What accounts for the attachment bond and the level of trust and security the infant and then the child develop comes from the daily back-and-forth of the parent and child (what Harvard's Jack Shonkoff calls the "serve-and-return" between parent and child and I refer to as "the dance"). These ongoing interactions embody the attachment relationship and enable parents to be the hidden regulators of their child's emotional arousal. In the daily interactions, the parent helps the child handle the ups and downs of arousal throughout the day; Hofer refers to this as a parent's "co-constructive skills"—those physical and verbal interactions that serve at least two purposes: soothing and calming a child while at the same time reinforcing healthy neurobiological wiring. The child is more or less depending on and using the parent's brain to help regulate emotions until theirs is more fully formed and able to regulate on their own. At an emotional and psychological level, the love and care received in these ongoing interactions is what shapes the child's inner knowledge that they are safe and cared for. Feelings of safety constitute both that they are okay and that they deserve to be taken care of. The loving, respectful back-and-forth of holding, feeding, attending to when crying, the routines of going to sleep and waking up, and eating are all behaviors that reinforce the intimate bond between caregiver and infant and continue to help the child develop optimally.

Over time, the child will learn to regulate more and more independently, meet their own physical needs, and manage their own emotions (mostly), based in the context of this foundational attachment relationship. We see this as children learn to turn to a teddy bear to hug when going to sleep, when they ask to listen to music that is calming and enjoyable, when they begin to say they're hungry or achy and initiate seeking out help; they are showing an emerging awareness of their own needs. And yet it is a lengthy road to doing this solely on their own; they are still dependent on you, the caregiver, throughout growing up, ever more at a distance over time.

Being Their Container and Anchor

And this is what we as parents and caregivers provide for our children: we develop a relationship that both contains and anchors their experience and scaffolds the process through which they develop the inner resources of resilience, so that when they are ready to separate and become independent, they have the inner know-how to manage stress and adapt to changing circumstances.

How do you become their anchor and container?

You do this by building a relationship with your child or teen that is consistent and flexible. It's a relationship that asks you to stay present and attuned and adjust your dynamic with them as they grow and mature and go through life changes. We know our children are not babies or little forever, and that we have to face the reality that they will eventually grow up, leave our nests, and create lives of their own (still connected to us more distally, we hope). There is a gradual letting go that happens over this long journey with them. I believe that is every parent's wish: for their child to become capable as an independent person and thrive on their own—although if yours are still very little, it may be hard to even fathom this future goal right now.

While your child is growing and developing, your relationship shifts to respond to them in age-appropriate, supportive ways dependent on their current needs; throughout this time, there also will be environmental factors that impact your relationship, including the daily and ongoing stressors. During stressful times, as well as during milder, everyday changes, it is your relationship with your child that will continue to help them feel grounded and capable. This will be the case even when you do not feel so grounded yourself. Your relationship with your child is what supports and steadies them, the container in which you hold them. It's not precisely you that's the container as if you are simply present to absorb their ups and downs so they don't feel the impact; rather, your relationship functions as a safe space where they feel held emotionally. At the same time, it's your relationship that anchors them, acting as a secure base to which they can return for comfort and care when needed.

Your relationship is the connection the two of you build over time and through your many interactions and shared experiences. And just as your relationships with friends and siblings and even a partner or spouse changes, so, too, will your relationship with your child. You also play a central role in what they carry within them and internalize as their model for relationships with others in their lives and how they grow to trust themselves. Even my college-age children call home to touch base, or for a check-in. It is different in its content and yet not so different from the school-age child waiting for the parents to come home after work or to pick them up from sports practice and then feeling relieved and secure to be together again. Parents are their children's home base.

The ways in which we as parents meet children's needs, however, are dynamic because their needs keep shifting. How we respond becomes increasingly nuanced depending on our children's needs of the moment, and gets more indirect over time. We step back to figure out what our children need from us as they grow through the elementary years into their teenage years and young adulthood. While children walk (and at times seemingly strut) the path of independence or push to keep separating to a greater degree, they simultaneously want, expect, and need parents to reorient in relation to them. Think of a line of string between you and your child: When your child is a baby, the tension of the string is lovingly held steady and tight, as you stay in close proximity. As your infant then child grows, you tend to loosen the string, allowing for some distance, but remain able to tenderly tug on the string to remind your child that you are still present, just out of hands' or eyes' reach, but close by, so to speak, for when they need you. Your child tugs on the string when they need you to come closer, allowing you to understand their needs and respond to them. It is a two-way set of pulling on and releasing of the string, allowing flexibility in the string's tension. Teenagers and young adults also benefit from this connection: yours may yell loudly and vociferously for you to "Leave me alone" or "Get out of my room" or "Stop hovering; I don't need you"—and while all of these exclamations reflect their desire at that moment for privacy, more distance, and independence, they also want you to be there, close enough, when they do need you, even if it is later on (and can happen suddenly). In other words, the string gets longer and looser, but it's still there, connecting the two of you, with variations in tension signaling the child's needs. Yes, even teenagers tug on that string, often when you least expect it. No doubt, it can get confusing.

As if this were not enough change to consider, relationships also vary with each of our children. There's no one parental playbook that can direct us on how to build the best relationship; there is no such concept. This may sound obvious, but it is still worth noting that relationships are made up of two distinct people interacting with distinct past histories and ever-changing needs to be met. We may find ourselves similar in temperament or personality with one child, with whom we communicate easily and fluidly. You may experience another child as wholly different from you and have a harder time "reading" or relating to that child, understanding what they want, or responding to their needs. One child may like physical closeness; another may prefer that you don't touch their hair or rub their back, unless they ask for it. One child may be the type of student you were—focused and diligent and cares a lot about their grades; another child may rarely bring home homework or may seem unmotivated by grades, preferring to spend time dancing, playing video games, rebuilding computers, or collecting bugs. The way you lovingly interact with each of these siblings will vary: Two different children; two different ways in the world. Two different people in relationship with you.

CHAPTER 2

The You Factor

We are all the products of our pasts, amalgamations of our experiences and upbringings—the good, the bad, what we treasure from it and what we wish were different, what we value and what we never had. The accomplishments and challenges we faced during our own childhoods, as well as unresolved disappointments and losses, affect who we are as parents. Some of us experienced loving, caring parents and an overall warm or supportive upbringing. Others of us have histories that are more complicated, marked or defined by painful experiences, including abuse, neglect, rejection, or loss. Many of us have a combination of some good and some bad experiences. Regardless of our individual history, we bring this background into our parenting, and are often unaware of its effect on our relationship with our children.

We all do our best as parents, but the events of our own childhood and past experiences can surface suddenly, seemingly out of the blue. If you recall strict rules that you resented as a child, you may find yourself wanting to be more flexible. If you felt chaos or lack of guidance in your home growing up, you may veer toward more order and control in your own parenting. You may be driven to replicate the loving, warm family get-togethers you had with extended family and cousins. Or you may be surprised by how you avoid family gatherings, which you only remember as painful or lonely, and prefer to form a family of friends from your child's school or your neighborhood or community. Many of us have chosen families of friends we gather with to celebrate and share our lives with who are not actual relatives.

As you become more attuned to both your individual child's needs and how best to be their container and anchor, you will naturally begin to reflect on aspects of your own experience that you want to bring into your relationship with your child and what you may not wish to repeat or want to outright avoid.

This collective personal history of relationships and family dynamics matters because it plays into how we relate to and interact with our children on a daily basis as well as messages we convey to them about people, themselves, and life. It affects our expectations about what makes them happy, how we think they should act, and what we define as goals for them. Our past also impacts our confidence and nagging doubts of ourselves as parents and our beliefs about our abilities to be there for our children. The past is an important context to be mindful of when managing our responses to our children and our ability to help them regulate. Becoming aware of your own intentions and issues takes time and does not always feel comfortable. In fact, it can feel deeply uncomfortable to recognize these parts of ourselves. Often, when parents come to me with issues related to their children, our discussions reveal that the heart of the problem lies more with unexamined thoughts, feelings, and beliefs of the parents rather than anything "wrong" with the child.

Here's an example. Jalyn, a young mother, described herself as being an unlikeable child and worried her daughter Claire would be, too. I asked what she meant by "unlikeable," and Jalyn recalled a vivid story from when she was eight: Jalyn's so-called best friend insisted she be the "servant to my friend's Queen of Sheba," who would bark commands and Jalyn would comply.

"I was pathetic. I just let her order me around, but she was my only reliable friend, and I so badly wanted her to like me, so I did whatever she said."

Now Jalyn seemed overly worried that her nine-year-old daughter would be treated meanly by other children just as she had been.

I asked her what about Claire's situation was causing Jalyn to worry, wondering if there was any evidence that Claire was lonely or had trouble making friends.

"I keep telling her to use her voice. I want her to have friends but not be bossed around, to have genuinely two-way friendships."

This sounded like valid advice, but I was still not sure what was troubling this mom. And then Jalyn said more: anytime Claire came home from fourth grade to report disagreements or problems with friends, even small ones, Jalyn blurted out, "Kids are so mean! They are just so mean! You have to protect yourself."

Despite wishing the opposite for her daughter, Jalyn was unintentionally allowing her past painful experiences to convey the message to her child that kids are mean and to avoid them.

In Jalyn's case, she was layering her experience onto her daughter, instead of being able to listen to exactly what may or may not have been troubling her daughter. It turned out that Claire was merely wanting to share the ups and downs of the friendship drama at school; her mother had jumped to the conclusion that Claire was being hurt by mean girls based on her own childhood peer experiences.

Here's another example. Reuben was an older father, having had his first child at age forty-seven. When he was a child, home was not a pleasurable or warm place. His parents worked long days, sometimes working more than one job to make ends meet. They were financially strained, and his father often came home exhausted and frequently short-tempered. Although he felt loved by his father, his father had little time for him, and Reuben did his best to avoid his father's anger. His mother was busy with his younger siblings after her own long day of work. Home was not a comforting place to be, so Reuben spent most of his free time playing outside with friends. He shared with me that his happiest memories are of the long bike rides he took with his friends and the elaborate games they created and played together. To this day, Reuben stays in touch with these friends, and now that he is a father, he sees making friends as a priority for his own children. He encourages their friendships and is a willing driver to activities with their friends. His twelve-year-old son Arturo is quiet and kind and prefers spending time with his mom and Reuben on the weekends, helping in the house or doing yard work together. When Reuben encourages, even pushes, Arturo to hang out with his friends, Arturo declines and insists on spending time with his parents at home. This clash between them often ends up with the two arguing about why Arturo doesn't want to be with friends.

Although it was clear to me that Reuben wants what's best for his son, he's not yet aware that he's basing his son's happiness on his own experience and overlooking what might work for his child. After all, Arturo is growing up in a warm, loving home that they created, different from the home life Reuben recalled.

Another common example of parents' unwittingly projecting their experience or histories onto their children occurs when they assume their children's interests and paths into adulthood align with their own, simply because they are their children. That was true for Alina and her brother, who were born in the US to immigrant parents from Asia. Their parents sent both their children to highly academic and competitive high schools on scholarship and expected them to excel (nothing less than an A was acceptable), following the same high-standards academic path into and through college.

Alina, now a parent herself, told me, "The whole reason my parents came here was to get the best education for their children. Their motto was 'work hard, do well in school, and get into the best name college you can reach,' whatever that was." Alina noted that her parents never considered her interests and neither did she. "After all, they sacrificed a lot to make this happen for us," Alina reflected.

I asked Alina if she had enjoyed her experience at her small, competitive liberal arts college, and she admitted, "Well, not really, I felt like I had no choice, but I would never have done anything different. My parents were very pleased."

And her brother? He was channeled into a science field at an elite university, was unhappy throughout, but never changed his major or career path, fulfilling his parents' dream of becoming a doctor. "You would think this was ideal since he is a successful and well-known physician," she commented, "but he is so resentful of all their pushing for so many years that he rarely sees them and for years refused to speak to our father."

Now, Alina's eleventh-grade daughter was balking at going directly to college, wanting instead to pursue a music career first, and her son wanted to become an environmental activist, working for an NGO. Alina came to me, upset with what her children were choosing to do with their lives. She exclaimed, "I gave them everything they need to succeed, and I worry that they are throwing it all away."

I pointed out that what she helped her children do was to find a path they were passionate about that included developing genuine interests; that they may indeed "succeed" still—just not via the same path that she or her brother had followed. We discussed that as a child her own dreams or passions were never nurtured or valued. Gradually, Alina became more aware of how she was still very much steeped in a mindset carved out for her by her own parents and shaped by their experience of coming to this country, and without realizing it, she had projected this onto her own children. When she began to reflect on her sadness about not having been able to have a say in choosing her college and career path, she slowly came to accept the desires of her children for their own pathways. She even began to admit that she liked their ability to think for themselves and begin to direct their own futures. She saw their passion as a positive attribute and recognized it was something she wanted for herself.

This is what I mean by the You Factor—what every one of us as parents brings to our role as a parent, no matter what background we come from. It is part of being human. Becoming aware of how these factors affect your relationship with your child is crucial to seeing your child for who they are, without the internal and often unconscious biases. Blocking out the child before you; setting up unrealistic expectations; or inadvertently judging or shaming their choices are threats to your connection and the trust your child will have in you.

Becoming Aware

Yet another example of how your past can creep into how you relate to your children comes from an email I received from a parent of two children who attended the Toddler Center several years ago. Debra was upset and confused by a situation that happened with her children who were in elementary school. Kara was now seven years old and in second grade, and her younger brother, Oliver, was in first. I remembered that the siblings had always been close, and I was eager to hear an update on how they were doing. I arranged a meeting where Debra described a recent visit to a science museum with Kara and Oliver, along with another mother and her two children. The siblings were happy to be with their friends, and all four were getting increasingly excited and rambunctious, which made Debra anxious since they were in a museum. As she felt herself getting more upset with their behavior, she tried to get them to behave by shushing them and otherwise trying to stop and quiet them. Her friend didn't seem to be distracted by the children's behavior, smiling back when Debra had given her a plaintive look.

When Oliver and his friend decided to run and slide on the shiny and slippery marble floor, Debra was exasperated and grabbed Oliver tightly by the wrist and gave it a tug, leaning in and, with gritted teeth, telling him to "Stop this now!"

Then, looking at the other mom, who had seen it all, she sternly admonished her children.

In a rush of embarrassment and heated anger, Debra turned to her friend to say that she was taking her kids home and abruptly (and unhappily) left the museum with them. It was an unpleasant ending to what had been until then an enjoyable outing.

There's a lot going on in this scenario, so let's unpack it. Before Debra's interference, the children seemed to be having fun in an exuberant fashion that rattled Debra. "Were the children behaving badly?" I asked Debra.

"Not really, but I thought they should be behaving better, less riled—we were in a public place, a museum," she insisted.

Debra was clearly the one who was uncomfortable with the rowdiness. Her friend was okay with it. It is not hard to sympathize with Debra: we all want our children to behave well in public places. And yet, Debra was most upset by how harshly she responded to what she now considered "normal child behavior," even though she did not like it.

Debra quietly asked me, "Why was I so bothered by the situation? Why was I so hard on my children?" with a clear desire to understand herself better.

"You mean by Oliver's exuberant excitement?" I asked.

"Yes—I thought he should be better behaved, but now I also realize he is a little kid."

"True, he's six years old. When you think about it, how many times has he been to a museum? Did he understand your expectations for what he could do or how he needed to behave while there?"

She hesitated and thought about it. "No—probably not. I guess

I could have been more clear, especially because he and his friend almost always get wound up together. But why did I grab him so hard like that?"

This is always the question to ask yourself: Why does a particular behavior or response of your child's get under your skin or push you to act more forcefully than usual? Because her reaction was so upsetting to her, I asked, "Is there anything in your background that you think made you feel so uncomfortable and so upset?"

She quickly responded, "I have thought about this before: my dad was in the military. He had a very strict set of rules for behavior in our family. My sisters and I were expected to be extremely well-behaved at all times or we'd get a literal slap on the wrist, sometimes more. Even his stern look was enough to keep us in line."

I asked if she wanted to use this strict approach for her own children, and without missing a beat she emphatically stated, "No, no, I don't want that at all! I don't want my children to fear me. But the part I do want is respect. We respected our father."

As we spoke further, Debra noted that maybe fear was not actually respect. And that left her wondering how her children would come to respect her if she was not strict. She also recognized that her strong reaction at the museum came from a place of feeling her children were being disrespectful—of the place, the people, and mostly, of her. She realized that her approach and expectations overlooked how young they were and that being tired at the end of their time at the museum probably was a recipe for getting wired up.

Over the next several months Debra worked on understanding her own hurt as a child, wanting her father's attention but not wanting to upset him. She became able to see her children as little people figuring out how to be in the world. She became more aware of when she was quick to anger and more discerning of the times when her children pushed her so-called buttons, like when they ran through the house and didn't listen to her, or if they became overtly loud or physical, wrestling and tumbling, for instance. She also figured out that her tolerance and patience lessened at times of transition, such as leaving the house or another place, like the museum; coming to the dinner table; or getting ready for bed. Once Debra identified the "hot spots," she worked intentionally to center herself at these moments. By being more grounded and calmer herself, she could support her children and help them better handle the transitional moments and their intense emotions, too. (Later in this chapter, you will find specific strategies for calming both yourself and your children during times of transition and other "hot spots.")

Grown-Ups Need to Regulate, Too

Knowing ourselves includes being aware of our emotional experience. Before we can even begin to help our children manage their own emotions, we first need to manage ourselves. When we cannot manage our own reactions or emotions, we are unable to help our children stay grounded. Bringing down their upset state depends on us being reasonable and calm. Maybe you did not have the best grounding yourself as a child and it's difficult for you to manage your emotions; now as a parent, you find yourself at one extreme or another—either agitated and angry or withdrawn and afraid to get involved—so instead you shut down. Perhaps there were upheavals in your life, trauma, or extended periods of stress that now affect your inner resources to deal with complicated or intense emotions. Perhaps your relationship with your own parents was fraught, lacked a sense of safety, or both. Now, with your own child, you feel overwhelmed and uncertain about how best to help them regulate, especially when faced with their intense emotions or behavioral upheavals.

Take, for example, a mother who is late to a family birthday party. She, her spouse, and their two children have rushed to get out the door and into the car. Throughout the morning and afternoon plans were being made, and the party was talked about. The children were getting more and more excited to see their cousins. But the mom has also gotten more anxious to see one of her siblings, with whom she's had an argument. The two haven't spoken in several months.

Now the back seat is heating up with giggles. When one child pulls the other's hair or pokes them (as a joke) in the belly, causing the other to squeal, the mom erupts in the front seat, letting out a loud, "Stop it!" in a stronger-than-typical voice and nearly swipes at them. Instantly, both children halt their behavior and start crying. It does not help that the mother is already on edge and nervous about seeing her sister. Now she is even more upset.

Suddenly the car is heated with negative emotion.

So what is the mother really upset about in this situation? Is it about the children poking and prodding and screaming? Is it her own pent-up emotions, tied to the anticipation of seeing her sibling and all that goes with this complicated relationship?

This example is a snapshot of how complicated competing or clashing emotions can play out with our children. While this exact situation may not apply to you, you may be able to come up with a similar situation for yourself when you were on edge, tense, or stressed and your child's behavior is what pushed you over the edge. You lost it. We often experience feelings and have reactions in response to others . . . not just to what's going on in our own heads.

I'm not here to judge the parent who loses her cool in the front seat (or at home)—she's anxious, she's upset, and I've been there, too; you may have been as well. But let's look at the situation as a common parenting predicament, in which we are dealing with more than one set of feelings (or emotional responses) at a time. How do we best manage our own feelings and remain in our "adult shoes"?

The woman in this situation could be reacting to any number of thoughts or feelings. Perhaps she and her sister have always had a tense relationship that now has left a lack of trust and some bitterness in its wake, or a loving relationship but one tinged with constant competitiveness. In either case, the woman's short-tempered response to her kids sparring in the back seat could have conjured up not-so-distant memories of when she and her sister fought as young girls. It would make sense that this history makes the woman more sensitive and more reactive, even though she is unaware of what underlies her reaction.

Or perhaps this mother is simply exhausted after a long week juggling work and kids and making doctors' appointments for her mother, so instead of schlepping to a family birthday party, she'd rather stay home, enjoy time with her children, and read a book or binge-watch a new series that evening with her partner. And although she and her sister argued the last time they were in the same room together, they are not close, so she's not really angry about that. She simply wants some peace and quiet in the back seat.

In this case, the woman's quick "Stop!" is loud but not angry; rather, it's a kind of cry for what she needs—to just stop because her nerves are frayed after a long, tiring week.

In either case, the children may not be hugely impacted, but how can we as parents learn to check our own feelings and reactions, so we have the bandwidth to help our children manage their own typical but challenging behavior and emotions? This is the precise conundrum of staying regulated ourselves so we can help our children learn to regulate on their own.

Let me point out: there is not necessarily a right way nor only one way for parents to manage such situations or learn to provide the support children need when emotions run high. We do have a range of options. The key is the need to be aware of these options so we can choose one. Underlying our ability to respond in helpful ways to any situation with our children taps into our own capacity to be flexible—not just when our lives and the time with our children are going swimmingly but particularly when stress sets in or heats up during times of uncertainty and high-pressure situations. The mom who kind of lost it in the car didn't intend to shout and almost swipe at her children; nor did she intend to make them cry. In fact, I'd bet that in either scenario, the mom felt pretty lousy about the situation getting so heightened from her response.

So how might the situation have been handled differently?

Perhaps she could have been more direct and told her spouse she didn't want to go to the family party.

Or she may have called her sister in advance and talked through the reasons behind their disagreement. Or even have called a friend to talk it through and get support before she went to the party. Or perhaps she might have steeled herself for the event and practiced a mindfulness exercise such as deliberate breathing to calm herself and remind herself she could handle the party.

Or she may have calmly and clearly turned around to her children in the back seat and asked them to cool it, telling them that it would be better and more enjoyable if everyone got along for the ride.

We always have options, but we do need to practice remembering them in the heat of the moment. The more emotionally charged the moment, the harder that will be, so we have to start with managing ourselves first, which is not always easy.

James Gross, a psychology professor at Stanford and an expert on emotion regulation, defines "emotion regulation" as "the processes by which individuals influence which emotions they have, when they have them, and how they experience and express them." Early on, psychologists studying regulation thought that all we needed to do to manage our emotions was either put a lid on these feelings or analyze them—both of which are cognitive/thinking processes. The reality, scientists have since discovered, is that regulation is very much a two-way interaction between these suddenly felt emotions and the more consciously controlled cognitive areas of the brain housed mainly in the prefrontal cortex. It's both bottom-up and top-down: the emotions arise (from the "bottom") and we learn how to handle them ("top"). Simply put, when we are in the midst of handling our emotions, the unconscious, emotional parts of our brain are communicating with the more intentional decision-making parts of our brains. When we get caught up in a powerful emotional surge—anger, jealousy, frustration, or intense pain/grief—our emotions are taking over; when we are able to notice that our children in the back seat are getting to us, and we can decide how to respond to the situation to more effectively manage it, we are engaging the decision-making, thoughtful part of our brain.

How does this interplay between emotion and cognition play out in real life? When we are anxious, for example, we have more difficulty staying emotionally regulated. We may feel more vulnerable and sensitive to criticism, more insecure and easily upset, or more likely to lash out if we feel threatened. Anxiety puts our emotions on edge, often leading to anger. In times of uncertainty, such emotions are always more heightened. Think again of emotions as states of arousal that we have the ability to tamp down or feed and heighten. Emotion regulation starts when we can identify the feeling as either positive and helpful or negative and destabilizing. This first level of appraisal, which happens quickly, will then begin to set off our go-to ways of dealing with those feelings, with some people being better able to manage the discomfort of their negative feelings, while others feel more easily upset or aroused.

When it comes to the parent-child interactions around emotion regulation, things can get tricky. Effectively reducing heightened emotional arousal at the biological and behavioral level increases a child's ability to manage frustration in the face of social and academic challenges, manage potential anxieties, and control thoughts and behavior, all of which are necessary for navigating the school context, eliciting positive social interactions, mental health, and adaptive functioning. Thus, effective emotion socialization strategies that foster the development of biobehavioral emotion regulation abilities are critical. It's also important to bear in mind that this learning process takes place over many years for a child, and the learning unfolds within the relationship with you.

Being Good Enough

The ways in which your child learns to deal with their emotions are clearly tied to how you deal with your own; the two go hand in hand. As the examples in this chapter suggest, how you feel and what you bring into the role of being a parent matter and play a central role in your manner of handling situations with your child or children. It's tempting to think that, because we are adults, we are fully in control of our emotions, but often emotions overtake us in an instant and automatic process that we do not expect. You won't always handle your own emotions well in response to your children. Given the vulnerable position our children's actions can unknowingly throw us into, it's no wonder that we lose track of how we feel or what we project onto a situation. Maybe you are even surprised by your reaction at times; I certainly have been. This is an element of being a parent that few of us knew about prior to becoming a parent, and yet, it is imperative to know who we are and what we bring to this intimate and important journey. Your upbringing, your experience, and even your relationship with your spouse or partner will affect your relationship with your child. These complex and varied pieces that we carry within us as parents also impact our effectiveness at helping our children learn to handle emotions and life on their road to developing resilience, kindness, and a solid sense of self.

So what does this mean for us in relation to our children? When we take the time and space to do the intentional work (that is not always going to be easy!) to understand ourselves and become aware of our own histories and emotional landscape, including disappointments and what we wish we had as children, we become more capable of being safe, attuned, connected caregivers to our children and building authentic relationships with them. By no means is this a mandate of perfection, as if you are at a child's beck and call. Nor am I suggesting that there is only one right way to be a parent (there is not). There are many ways to show love and support. Indeed, back in the 1950s, the highly regarded pediatrician and psychoanalyst D. W. Winnicott introduced the theory of good-enough mothering, which means exactly what it sounds like: when parents are "good enough," the child is able to get their essential needs met and is accepted for who they are, including being a person who gets angry and has other negative emotions. When this happens, they feel safe enough to leave their parent's side and explore the world. Winnicott wrote about mothers, who were considered the only important parent at that time, but we know that mothers and fathers both matter to the child, and that either one or both or another primary caregiver can meet a child's needs and give the clear message that they are available to the child, caring, and attuned.

Beyond highlighting the concept of perfection, he went further to raise the alarm on the potential dangers that striving to be perfect can do. Winnicott believed that the idea of perfection in parenting was harmful and that as the infant grows into a child, they need to see that their parent is, in fact, not perfect. When a parent does not meet a child's needs every once in a while, the child is forced to adapt and thereby grow resilient. I want parents to hold in mind this idea that striving for perfection is not only unrealistic, it also robs your child of an opportunity to build resilience.

Let's face it. It's okay to have our feelings—good, bad, and ugly. It's also okay to let our children know this in age-appropriate ways. When we are in an authentic relationship with our child and raising them to be resilient, decent human beings, they need to know that we are not perfect nor striving to be so. Winnicott recognized that the parent-child relationship prepares a child for life, and that in the relationship's natural disruptions and a parent's mistakes, children learn to adapt and adjust. In a healthy, imperfect relationship with you, your child learns how relationships truly work.

I emphasize Winnicott's writings because after decades of experience with parents and children, I heartily agree. The hard part for you, the parent, is to accept your own faults and missteps and come to a place where loving care is good enough. When you drop perfection, you can move to being your child's container and anchor: being flexible and not hard on yourself and interacting without judgment. The relationship is the dance between the two of you, and the steps will be smooth sometimes and other times not; the two of you are in this together for the long haul.

In the next part of this book, I will share practical strategies for not only helping your child build resilience but also how you can nurture a long-lasting authentic relationship with your child or children. The five pillars will be your guideposts as you practice maintaining healthy boundaries and setting reasonable limits so that your child internalizes that important sense of emotional safety. And by staying self-aware and shedding your own shame and worries, you will be able to see the wonder of the child in front of you, support their best development, and let them know you are there for them, even in the hardest times.

• • •

REFLECTIVE QUESTIONS

Bring to mind a situation that made you feel an intense emotion: angry, frustrated, deeply sad or confused, jealous; it could also be pride, excitement, or happiness. Then take some time to consider the following questions:

- Was the situation negative or positive?
- How did you handle the situation and the accompanying emotions? How did you react?
- Looking back, how do you feel about the way you responded? Do you wish you had responded in a different way? How would that have been?
- How do you typically respond to stress or stressful situations? How do you typically respond to intense emotions or the potential for intense emotions?
- What are some of the scenarios that make your own emotions and arousal system become heightened? Are there familiar moments or situations that get you upset? Are there situations when you cut off emotions or try to avoid them?
- What helps you calm down? Are there strategies that help you regain your inner balance or sense of groundedness?
- What do you recall from childhood that you hope to replicate with your child and family? What do you recall that you aim to do differently?

Whatever your answers to these questions, being aware of your responses and reactions to stressful moments is a key component of being able to regulate your emotions and keep yourself grounded. The more aware you are of these processes and what you bring, positive and not so positive, from your childhood, the better able you will be to help your child thrive.

PART II

The Five Pillars of Your Child's Resilience

Using the Five Pillars of Resilience

When I teach courses on typical and atypical child development, I break down the developmental areas of a child's growth into buckets, categorizing them according to types of needs—from physical (biological) to emotional (psychological), social to cognitive (intellectual), as if each area were separate and developing in its own little bubble. I do this so that we can think about the importance of each area in its own right, discuss the research addressing one domain or another, and unpack the importance of the area for the developing child. In actuality, these developmental areas within the child work in tandem and overlap.

When I teach, I explain that though we will talk about the areas as separate, we will put them all back together into the actual and more complex model of development. One area impacts another in an intricate interplay of mutual influences because children develop as whole beings, not as separate parts. In order to understand whole child development, looking at the separate areas helps to hone in with a focused lens on each area that drives the process of children growing into and becoming themselves. I take a similar approach in communicating the beauty and intricacy of a child's development or challenges to parents. By unpacking these pieces, I can illuminate how your unique relationship with your child acts as the consistent and steady container and anchor for supporting them through all of development.

The five pillars discussed in this section reflect these developmental areas; they also align with the skills we can both teach our children directly and through our relationship with them so they can build the inner resources of resilience to last them throughout their lives. The internalization of a secure base, self-regulation, the development of agency and independence, social intelligence and compassion, and inner self-love and acceptance sync with the core milestones of child development and give you the opportunity to support and reinforce what children need to become autonomous, confident people, able to adapt and bounce back day in and day out as well as during times of a lot of uncertainty or high stress. So while I lay out the pillars separately in the forthcoming chapters, they overlap and reinforce one another and do not require a linear progression. You can start with any one of the five pillars and move on to other relevant pillars as it suits your needs.

In pillar one, "Learning to Trust," you will build and help reinforce a sense of safety in your relationship with your child, responding to their most basic needs and attuning to them with nuance as they grow and mature; with this foundation, your child can trust and count on you, and then, over time, develop an inner sense of safety and trust within themselves that will anchor them throughout their life. Whereas you are the anchor throughout their development, they gain the ability to anchor themselves, still in relation to others, as they grow.

In pillar two, "Learning to Regulate," you will help your child understand and manage their emotions. You begin by co-regulating their brain-body system alongside and together with them, which may sound complicated but is actually a process that is inherent to the relationship itself. You are already doing it every day. When children ultimately learn to self-regulate, they become capable of (mostly) managing their own behavior and emotions as they grow more and more self-aware.

In pillar three, "Developing Agency," you will see how and why giving children limits along with space and freedom is necessary as they begin the process of separation and then move toward increasingly greater independence. Though separation can get messy, happening in fits and starts, it is what enables children to develop agency, that inner capacity to make sound decisions and work toward goals.

In pillar four, "Connecting with Others," you will see how your relationship with your child serves as a model for how they in turn learn to connect authentically with others and develop important social skills. Social or interpersonal skills don't happen on their own; children need scaffolding and explicit teaching, so they learn how to get along with others, know how to respect boundaries (their own and those of others), and build authentic relationships.

Finally, pillar five, "Being Understood," shows you how in accepting your child and seeing them for who they are (which can be different from who you'd like or expect them to be), your child learns how to accept and love themselves. This happens when a child feels seen and understood in all their complexities. This pillar shows parents how to avoid the seeds of shame that can be so corrosive to a child's sense of self and instead simply and freely love them without reservation.

As you move through the pillars and test out some of the

suggested strategies, think about how the aspects of development and resilience overlap and support one another; also think about how the pillars and their strategies offer you ways to not only stay connected to your children as they grow and develop but also how to create "touchpoints" that deepen and solidify the relationship itself at all ages. This takes on increasingly more importance as children gain independence, spend more time outside of the family, and eventually move out on their own. Of course, how you and your child navigate the pillars varies quite a bit. A child may, for instance, develop physically quite quickly (e.g., learn to walk at ten months) but have a more timid personality, showing fear of new people in the social realm that remains present, even as it lessens, late into middle school. So it's important to keep in mind that, like development itself, the process of helping your child build these inner resources of resilience is never linear. And because you are teaching these skills within the context of your relationship, aspects of you will come into play—in intended and unintended ways.

With this in mind, you will find additional Reflective Questions to consider as you continue to grow alongside your child. The better we know ourselves as parents, the better we can be as parents. The questions are meant to support your becoming aware of what sets you off and why it sets you off; your expectations and whether they are realistic; your goals for your children; and your beliefs and values. "Know thyself, as best you can" will be a guiding theme as you think about what your child needs now and far into the future.

A realistic through line to also keep in mind is the inevitability of change and disruption in small and large ways, and how these moments and times of uncertainty are indeed natural opportunities to dig in and use what we already know about children's needs. Ultimately, of course, we want our children to be able to handle transitions, life's ups and downs, and upheavals for themselves, as you move into the background more over time. And yet, how they learn to build these capacities will depend heavily on how you interact with them at any given point. As noted before, the daily moments of connection and interaction, even on your simplest, smoothest day, increase the capacity to buffer and build the strengths for the tougher and more challenging moments that will surely arise.

CHAPTER 3

The Safety Net

Pillar One: Learning to Trust

When we consistently attune to our children and communicate the message that they can count on us, we help them internalize the knowledge that they are safe. This feeling of safety and the knowledge that they are not alone in the world grounds them in everyday moments of uncertainty and upset and supports them as they move through life, encountering all types of difficult transitions, disappointments, and painful events. As parents, we have the power to confirm a child's inner sense of both safety and trust; the two go hand in hand to build an important pillar of resilience.

Once the initial attachment relationship with our children is established or reestablished, much of how we reinforce the gradual building of inner safety and trust happens through the overall quality and regularity of our daily interactions—our continued fulfillment of a child's basic needs of food, shelter, and love; attunement to their emotional ups and downs; establishment of routines; sensitive responses to the child during times of change and/or when outside forces disrupt the regular routines; and communication that helps children understand the events around them through narrative. The steadiness of our interactions communicates to a child that they are loved and valued and that they will be okay when changes occur, good and bad. When a child feels safe and trusts you, they are more likely to trust themselves to approach the world with curiosity, explore and test themselves, and build a strong sense of self that is agile and resilient.

On the contrary, without this inner sense of safety, children can become anxious and hypervigilant, monitoring every shift in their environment. They may be distracted and inattentive and become overly self-protective, ever watchful of their needs not being met or potential harm coming their way. When a child does not learn to trust a parent, they are in a constant search for a sense of safety that is not present and may ultimately develop a sense of self based on what they lack rather than their strengths, which in turn is a breeding ground for deep-seated shame.

Every child requires a sense of internalized safety before they can learn to fully self-regulate, separate from you as a step toward being independent, and form new relationships out in the world—all of which is both exhilarating ("I want to be out on my own!") and scary ("I don't want to be all by myself"). Children, regardless of their age, are drawn to novelty, while at the same time wrestling with fears of the unknown and risks that make them feel vulnerable. This push-pull between the need for safety and the desire to be out in the world is the space in which your containing and anchoring becomes so important. Often, when faced with the desire to try something new, children experience a clash of feelings—excitement to move forward (e.g., join the marching band, scale up a large climber, or walk to school on their own for the first time) and also anxiety. When parents help to steady them and be with them through their worries, fear, or doubts, you are showing them that they are not alone, that you are there to support them, and that they can count on you to get them through tough moments or prolonged stressful times. You are also showing them that they can have these intense feelings and come through them okay.

The main way that parents help build and reinforce a child's sense of safety is through regular attunement and consistency. An attuned parent is one who keeps their child's needs in mind, not on a twenty-four-hour basis but by connecting with them physically and emotionally in a regular way. It's not always easy to stay present—we are busy people; we have competing priorities; we get stressed, frustrated, and tired. We are human, after all. The good news is that children are flexible and forgiving when they are anchored by an overall loving and secure relationship. When a parent stays attuned, caring, and available as best they can, they enable the child to trust them as reliable and dependable, and able to meet their needs, most of the time. Eventually, the trust they experience with their parent is internalized and they learn to trust themself as well. This trust becomes a foundational resource of resilience: the knowledge that they are capable of managing change and uncertainty.

Be Responsive and Attuned

When parents anticipate and respond to a child's needs, the parent signals a profound message: "I see you, I hear you, I am here for you, you are safe." When a child receives this message again and again in varying circumstances, that message becomes part of the story they can tell themselves:

"I'm okay."
"Mommy knows."
"I'm not alone."
"Daddy cares."
"I am loved."

A parent's overall consistency and availability help a child learn to trust not only you, but themselves and other people as well; trust is a by-product of inner safety. Of course, this internalized sense of safety and trust does not develop overnight; it takes time to build with each daily interaction, reinforced over their years of upbringing and the sum of many, many exchanges between you and your child. Your relationship is built on this foundation and includes ups and downs, disruptions and disconnections, and the resets and repairs that bring you back together and return your child's inner sense of safety and equilibrium. Such breaks in connection don't have to be cause for alarm. Like I mentioned earlier, our children know inherently how to adapt to changing circumstances, but when we reinforce their sense of safety at such times, we strengthen the resilience factors that are taking root within our children.

Being responsive and attuned may seem intuitive, but it bears unpacking because, regardless of whether your child is three or fifteen, it can feel tricky when you are also trying to guide your child. Being attuned means you . . .

- Cue into your child's emotions and convey back your understanding.
- Accept your child's emotion without trying to change or dismiss it.
- Respond to your child's nonverbal cues by letting them know you're there: "Anything up?" "How are you doing?"
- Listen and respond to your child without judgment.
- Empathize with and validate your child's experience or feelings.

Staying attuned also means keeping your own feelings in check by staying aware of them so you can manage them in the moment. As children get older, you may find situations when your own experience is worth sharing with your older child, teen, or young adult.

Rely on Routines

Countless child-rearing books—from Dr. Spock to T. Berry Brazelton and Penelope Leach—have shown that routines help both parents and children fall into a rhythm, set the body clocks of babies and young children, and give parents much-needed breaks in between the physically demanding parts of child care in the early years. When our children are babies, most of us strive to stick to a routine because the feeding, diapering, and sleeping schedule is paramount to organizing our days and nights. We tend to think of routines as the structures we set up for our little ones, the "under fives," but routines are immeasurably important for children of all ages, as well as adults. Routines help ground us so that we can move through the day more automatically, freeing up energy to focus on goals or relax with more enjoyment.

While routines help organize our days, they are also what anchor us in times of turbulence and uncertainty; for this reason, they are often the first thing we put in place when something eventful happens. This was true in the early days of the pandemic shut down in 2020; it's true when you move to a new house or city or when families flee floods, fires, or earthquakes; it's also true when a loved one dies. Looking back on 2020, you may remember the outpouring of advice from teachers and psychologists to establish routines when many people were stuck at home. Routines for work, school, mealtimes, and sleep helped us simply get through the day. We had to create new ways of organizing our days and nights—from eating meals to doing school- and homework or working from home. These routines helped us feel like we had some control, when everything around us felt like it was swirling out of our control.

In another example, following the World Trade Center attacks in 2001, the families in a study I co-led of children who had directly witnessed the tragedy reported that after fleeing to safety, the most helpful thing they did was set up new routines. They found a new park or playground so their children could go outside and play like they always had. They established bedtime routines, even when they were in temporary places staying with friends or relatives. They bought foods familiar to their child. They wanted to provide comfort at a time when people were frightened, and routines provided a touchstone to what their children knew as familiar.

Establishing routines for eating, sleeping, and playing also ensures that your baby's or child's basic needs are met, and gives your growing child the opportunity—day in and day out—to learn to expect when to wake up and go to sleep, when to eat, and ultimately how to self-soothe and remain calm between these activities. Routines also provide times during the day and evening for you to engage and connect; they are opportunities for you to guide your children, show love and care, and talk and listen to them. In this way, routines become part of the texture of your relationship that continues as your child grows up; they act as regular opportunities to reinforce your connection and foundation of trust that underlies your relationship. If part of your morning routine or getting your baby dressed includes cooing and talking, smiling into a child's eyes, and playing with their fingers and toes, they come to expect this warm interaction and take it in positively. In this routine and loving daily interaction you are also communicating the safety message: *You are loved and cared for.* While these patterns and routines begin in infancy, the rhythm continues throughout development, though in slightly different ways.

The automatic flow of routines feels familiar, comforting, and empowering to children; knowing how the bedtime routine unfolds, where they do homework, and when to take a shower or bath grounds them, and they rely on you to establish and follow these routines. You likely know this because if one part of a routine is off, other parts can get thrown off, too. Did your seven-year-old forget to brush his teeth after breakfast? Then he may have also forgotten to grab his backpack. Such mishaps occur because routines lock us into certain patterns of behavior and when one step in the sequence is skipped or missed, others may follow.

Routines also provide opportunities for you to get to know an individual child and their unique ways and needs, and to note when these needs change. How does she respond when it is time to wind down? When a different parent puts him to bed? Our children vary in both obvious and nuanced ways: the one who readily adjusts to a change of place when we sleep at a grandparent's house; the one who needs the routine followed down to the detail or they have trouble handling their emotions. Routines expose valuable information and enable us to assess how our children are doing on any given day or during times of transitions. When you are in the midst of your routines throughout the day, whether that is getting two elementary-age children out the door or wishing your fourteen-year-old a good day as they flee off to school, you can begin to pay attention to and interpret what they are communicating to you: Is your infant sated from the meal? Does your seventh grader seem more anxious than usual? Is your five-year-old dawdling because going to school always makes them sad? Does your teenager seem reluctant to head out for band practice, which they usually love? These are important moments of the day to tune in to.

As children get older, keeping family routines tends to get more complicated, but even the most basic of them are still valuable as a way to provide grounding. As children grow more independent and their days become busier, you may not be able to sit down together for dinner at the same time every night, for example. Be realistic: if having nightly dinner as a full family is not always possible, figure out at least a few times per week that you can either gather together at a meal as a family or with one child. Shared meals provide good opportunities to check in and touch base.

As children grow, routines become more like rituals. Routines are what we do nearly without having to think in an organizing kind of way. Rituals are the next step, with a more focused intention and goal, such as wanting to be sure you have dedicated time with your tween and teenager each week, so you begin to have weekend brunch where you plan a menu, decide on a music playlist, and then cook together. The content of the ritual matters less than the coming together: it grounds children in the familiar and sets up regular expectations—even for distracted middle schoolers or sullen teens who balk at family movie night but plop down on the couch nonetheless. For years I left a snack and a note for my children when they came home from school as a connecting touchpoint that helped them bridge the school day with their return home; it also let them know I was thinking of them when I was still at work. The routine of coming home, putting their backpacks away, and watching some TV before doing homework or practicing piano remained. The ritual was the touchpoint of a snack and a note from Mom.

Consider these common times to establish routines for any task you do every (or most) day:

- Morning wake-up
- Getting dressed
- Mealtimes
- Leaving the house
- Bath/shower time
- Bedtime
- Heading out to school
- Homework
- Instrument practice
- Daily or weekly exercise
- Family entertainment night
- Weekend family time

As you create your own family routines and rituals, remember, too, to build in flexibility. When changes occur, which they inevitably do, flexibility is needed. Deviations from the routine might include:

- Friends coming for a sleepover
- Relatives visiting for an afternoon or a few days
- A parent being out of town
- A new after-school babysitter arriving
- A birthday being celebrated
- Illness or a visit to the ER

After these events, be sure to return to your set routines as they provide predictability that reinforces a sense of safety. They are the baseline touchpoints that we return to following the change. They also make life simpler because as routines become internalized and automatic, they free us up, allow for growing independence, and feel calming.

Help Make Meaning

Another way you act as container and anchor is by helping children make sense of their world. While this may sound obvious with younger children, it is another critical role you have with older ones as well. They look to you to help them understand what is going on around them, answer their questions, and explain underlying tensions or stressors. When a parent is away for work or when their school and the world closes down due to a virus called COVID-19, children need us to help them understand the connections between events and their lives so they don't make erroneous assumptions. I call this providing a narrative, and it's part of how we help our children feel safe in the world and, yes, stay grounded during times of high stress or uncertainty.

We do this kind of storytelling with our children quite naturally. When we chat to an infant, who we know doesn't understand the content of the words that we are saying, we are still sending little cognitive missives to our child's brain; the brain is taking in the chatter, its loving tone, and the visceral connection that "baby talk" communicates. Indeed, researchers have shown that children whose parents or caregivers talk to them build stronger verbal skills when they do start talking and then reading.

When children are young, they don't experience this narrative in an articulated way; they *feel* it. The loving tone of the narrative holds them and is an important way you act as their container. As children mature and put language to their feelings and experience, these messages begin to take shape as inner self-talk, what researchers call inner speech, which plays an important role in processes as diverse as memory, cognition, emotional regulation, and self-reflection. Inner narrative enables a child to understand themselves and develop theory of mind, the capacity to imagine and infer the state of mind of another person, which is related to the development of empathy and caring for others. (More on this concept in chapter six.) These understandings are absorbed in the very cells of their body via the circuitry in their brains. It may be difficult to imagine that our thoughts, beliefs, and feelings really do guide how our cells speak to one another in what scientists refer to as the brain-body connection. Psychologists call this process of moving from felt experience to the child's beliefs the process of internalization, and repeated patterns are key here. When parents engage children in this narrative building, they reinforce a vital skill of resilience: the ability to differentiate between what is happening in the world, what they see and are consciously aware of, and what is happening inside of them, their feelings and processes inside. They learn to depersonalize events instead of drawing conclusions that they caused something to happen. The danger here is that without an accurate narrative, children can blame themselves, thinking they must have done something bad to cause this negative event or outcome and causing them to feel ashamed. For example, they may infer that a parent being upset and yelling; a hurricane dislocating them from home; parents fighting with each other; or a friend not being at school one day was somehow their fault. This feeling of shame can linger and even become embedded in their sense of self. When you engage in narrative building, helping your child make meaning of events, you help them avoid this assumption of guilt and its resulting shame.

Your regular, daily communications also matter. One parent shared, "When my girls were little, I found myself talking about the plan of the morning or the day out loud, as a way to help prepare them for what was coming. My older daughter in particular really needed a heads-up—she did not like surprises. The younger one made transitions more easily—from home to the car was no big deal—whereas her older sister (even as a tween) needed at least one cue from me that 'in five minutes we are getting in the car.'" This kind of explicit talking helps explain the world to children for many reasons—to prepare them as in the example above; to connect the dots between an event that they may or may not know about and its impact; and to begin to help shape their understanding of their environment and their place in it. This knowing sense of what is happening helps them feel safe as well. This is an action you may already do with day-to-day events and changes. For example, "Today at school I heard there is going to be a new activity and you will be introduced to instruments in case you want to learn to play one," or "I will be late tonight, so I won't be home for dinner; I hope your math presentation goes well, and I look forward to hearing about it later."

Simple explanations with enough information, depending on their age, ground your child, make them feel safe, and reinforce their trust in you:

"It's raining outside, so we will need to bring an umbrella."

"The bus is late, so I will have to drive you."

"You may not be happy about this, but your friend had to cancel the afternoon activity with you. We will do it another time."

"Today is different because I can't pick you up from Grandma's; Daddy is going to pick you up today. I will see you at dinnertime."

"Maybe you heard people talking about something bad that happened today where people were hurt. I am wondering what you heard, and I will tell you what I know."

"An email went out today about the student at your high school. I want to hear what you are thinking about, and I'll share the information I have. It is no one's fault, but it is very upsetting."

"You know the virus I told you about? The doctors are trying to figure out how it spreads; until we know for sure, we want to be safe and wear masks. You'll see that all the kids and teachers at school are going to wear masks. I'll help you get used to it."

These bits of narrative about their lives become even more critical at times of stress and big changes, whether ongoing or sudden, such as when marital and family tensions arise, moves and other home changes occur, or a parent is away for work or becomes ill or injured. These narrative explanations send the message that your child can count on you to let them know what is going on, especially when the reality is hard to hear about, not readily understood, or something they might get upset about. Not saying anything or keeping information secret can work against their trust in you and subsequently undermine trust in themselves. The feeling that something is going on, but they do not know what it is, and not having a trusted adult verbalize the so-called elephant in the room can be destabilizing. Lucia is a great illustration of this. When her parents, Ron and Marisa, came to see me about nine-year-old Lucia, one of their four children, they were concerned about her quiet and increasingly withdrawn behavior. Yes, it was during a time when children were still online for school due to the pandemic, but they felt she had handled it well until this time and had been even more social online with friends. We went over what might be underlying this behavioral and mood change, but I could not identify anything with them that seemed different or impactful. Then I asked how they were doing; after all, this was many months into the pandemic and most of us felt stressed and unmoored.

Ron had been laid off for months and now was back to work. Money was tight. Marisa worked from home with three children attending school virtually and a baby. It had not been easy. Understandably, they reported high stress. I asked if they were arguing or fighting in front of the children. They told me that they "only fought in the other room, away from the children" and were sure that the children never heard them upset.

It took me a bit to help them see that as the most responsible of their children, sensitive and tuned in, as they described her, Lucia probably heard their fighting. In fact, she could be worried since she was feeling the tension, likely hearing them argue, and yet no one was talking about this openly. Things that remain unspoken are scary for children. I suggested they speak with her and the other children about the tensions and disagreements and let her know that it was not her fault that Mommy and Daddy did not always get along; explain that they argued sometimes, and it was hard to have everyone at home and a new job for Daddy, so sometimes even Mom and Dad had a hard time. I recommended they also tell her that Mommy and

Daddy still loved each other and would always take care of the children, even if they argued.

When they communicated this information, Lucia was visibly relieved and chimed in that this was like when she and her best friend had some fights, and they said they did not want to hang out together anymore. But then they both realized they really did want to be friends, and they came up with a plan to stop fighting.

"Yes," her dad noted, "this is similar. Even when two people love each other, we can still have times we don't get along."

The point here is that not talking about a problem in the family or an incident that affects your child can be worrisome to them, even scary. They may wonder why no one is talking about it (is it so bad that no one will even utter a word?), or they may not be sure of what they are feeling and experiencing, as when there is unexplained tension in the house or there are hushed murmurings about a world event. They can act out aggressively or melt down in response, unable to decipher the situation; their behavior is signaling that they understand something is wrong. Again, children will often blame themselves, as in, "I know something is wrong; I must have done something bad." Which can turn into, "I AM bad." Which rolls into feelings of shame. Rather than letting the vacuum make them think they are at fault, provide an age-level explanation and give them the opportunity to ask questions; providing this container will free them up with great relief. The narrative provides them a sense of "Oh, that is what is happening; now I know, even if I don't like it," while reiterating the reminder that you are there to care for them.

Another example is from when my youngest son was in middle school. He and a group of friends were meeting at our house to go trick-or-treating on their own. Earlier in the day there had been a horrific attack on a highly frequented bike path not far from where we lived. I weighed whether I should say anything about it to him or his friends. I wondered if they knew about it, and truthfully, I hoped they did not so they could be innocent kids out trick-or-treating. I monitored the situation as they gleefully dressed up for their time out together and we discussed rules about where they would go and when to be home. As they were walking out the door, my son turned back to me and blurted out, "Mom, did something bad happen today?"

I asked what he knew.

He repeated his question and said, "Just tell me."

I verified that yes, something bad had happened. "Did anyone get hurt?" he asked.

I said yes without saying anyone was killed (as he had not asked that). Then I assured him that there was no danger in our area and he could still go out with his friends. They skipped off. I had answered his question at that moment and had time to think about what to say later. What would the narrative be? I wanted to be both truthful and not overly scary.

Fast-forward: The children returned and excitedly sorted, ate, and exchanged candy. Then the friends left. It was now late and quiet when he said, "Please tell me what really happened."

I had to think through what I wanted to share with my almost teen, given that it was now bedtime. A child's age and developmental level and temperament always matter when providing an honest narrative that is both truth-laden and age-appropriate. I explained the situation and what had happened with a few facts. He asked two questions: Where did it happen? and Did people die? Earlier he was not ready to ask this (he was headed out for fun, and, appropriately, that was his focus). I verified that people had died, and others were hurt. I also let him know that the perpetrator was caught, and no one else would be hurt by him. I could see his relief, a feeling of safety even if what happened was bad. He then realized this was a path that we rode our bikes on, and we discussed how scary it was to know the place. I also informed him the path was closed for now and that when the parks and city officials reopened it, it would be made safe to ride again, all of which happened in time.

I was able to help create a narrative of the events by answering his questions, being truthful, and not providing any more information than I thought he could handle at the time. Thinking about what your child needs in that moment and providing a sense of safety (such as "the perpetrator was caught") are key, reminding them that there are people working to provide safety. I gave him enough information to make sense of what was going on and to help him make sense of what he would hear at school in the days that followed. I also knew that I had to remain open to more questions that might come, which they do, often at random and unexpected times. This is true when bad things happen locally in your community or in your family as well as in the broader world.

It's easy for busy adults to forget that children of all ages don't necessarily understand how things fit together nor understand what is happening around them. Yet when we as parents become a reliable, steady voice, we anchor and contain their experience. The anchor comes through our managing our own emotions and giving explanations that help them feel safe. The container is listening to their worries, noting their feelings, and providing extra attention or time together or physical comfort and cuddles, all in the aim of helping them make sense of the world so they don't have to feel overwhelmed by worrisome or frightening situations or feelings and giving them a safe space to handle their range of feelings.

Reset and Repair

Narratives are also part of a process of resetting when changes happen and repairing when disconnection between you and your child occurs. The predictability of the routines and patterns provides a safe baseline for your interactions and moving through each day. And yet, routines are not always consistent, which is okay because the occasional lack of consistency can turn into an opportunity for you to build a stronger relationship with your child. Disruption in routines and, similarly, disconnections in your relationship with your child will naturally happen and can be expected. A vital element of maintaining a loving, secure bond with your child is to understand how to reconnect when there's been a disruption in routines or a conflict or misunderstanding between you, which likely will happen more than you think. Think back to the earlier discussion of good-enough parenting, where perfection is not a healthy goal. What really matters is not the disconnecting incident, the disrupted routine, or the content of the conflict or upset; what matters is how you repair and reconnect with your child, and it's up to you to initiate.

I use the term "disruption" when referring to routines or changes in the children's lives that cause upset or instability. I use the term "disconnection" when there are breaches in your relationship with your child, small or large, including conflict or times of misunderstanding or miscommunication when the trusted bond between you gets severed or tested, and there is a need to repair that. Disruptions and disconnections come in all shapes and sizes, regardless of a child's age. Here are a few examples:

- Your child's favorite eighth-grade teacher ("The only one I really like!" she says) is going on maternity leave from school. Your daughter talks back to you when you try to explain who will fill in.
- The plans for the family weekend get-together are suddenly changed to the following weekend because a major work assignment means you have to work this weekend. The cousins are not coming to town as planned. Your eight-year-old

screams that you are the worst parent ever and asks why you always have to work.

- Daddy, who does the regular bedtime routine, is not going to make it home tonight to put your four-year-old to sleep. An epic tantrum ensues, especially because Daddy was also busy earlier in the week.
- You yell at your child for not listening or for stalling bedtime, accuse your teen of lying before knowing the full story, insult your child when you are tired of their talking back, or ignore the whining third grader to the point he is screaming at you to be heard and you are fully fed up.

Such situations are reminders that what might seem small or unimportant to us, and for which we may have a reasonable remedy— Daddy will do bedtime tomorrow; the cousins are coming next weekend—can be upsetting to your child, even if it seems minor to you. Stressful moments lead children to react, and any change of routine has the potential to be a stressful moment, again highlighting the benefit of our attuned presence. Even when children know the reason for changes, there will still be times when they become rattled, angry, or withdrawn. Their shifts in mood indicate they're uncomfortable with the change. Your relationship once again becomes their container and their anchor and an opportunity to allow their feelings (being the container) and reassure them that all is okay (being the anchor). Even if such disruptions are temporary, children can still feel an increased vulnerability that needs to be addressed in order to help them feel steady and safe again. Remember they look to you to help them adjust to the change in circumstance. It's important, for instance, that you explain why there's been a change in plans or reassure them that the routine being broken is not permanent: "This is just for today; tomorrow your teacher will be back," or "When Granddad leaves, you can go back to sleeping in your room again." Children benefit from explicit explanations, so they don't fill in the blanks in a self-blaming or otherwise harmful way. For example:

> *Explain the reason for the disruption.* "I did say I would be the one attending your middle school event. I got caught working late and thought it better to have Mommy come instead. I know how upset you are and what a big event this was. I am sorry; this is my mistake."
>
> *Repair the disconnection.* "Sometimes Mommy and I argue, and we disagreed today. Then we got mad and I yelled at you. That is not your fault; we should not yell like that. We worked it out and we still love each other and love you, but I know that was scary. I am sorry we were so upset and that I yelled at you, and we will try to be better at getting along."

When an incident is recognized for what it was, such as an accident, a sudden change that was upsetting or distracting, a misunderstanding, or an unintentional mistake that you know is disappointing to your child, they will use your cue to settle and move on, even if they need some time. Both the explanation for the disruption and/or the repair are a relief, as they are reminders that mishaps happen and the connection between the two of you can be restored.

Here's another example of how to handle a disruption in a child's routine. Say you receive an email explaining that your kindergartener's teacher will be out today, the day his teacher had designated your child as calendar helper. When you convey this change to your child, he gets quiet and is clearly disappointed. The next thing you know, he is sitting on the floor and refusing to put his boots or jacket on to leave for school. What happened to your easygoing five-year-old? His excitement for the morning routine was interrupted by the news that his teacher is going to be out. Addressing the disappointment openly and providing reassurance that he will get another turn as the calendar helper may be enough to move him from home to his scooter and then to school. By giving him this narrative, he may still feel disappointed, but in acknowledging his experience, you've given him the support and the space to move on and adjust—the essence of resetting and repairing.

When you initiate a repair, you are teaching your child a valuable lesson about the nature of relationships: they are not either/or, all or nothing. Just because the two of you have a disagreement, experience hurt feelings, or exchange hurtful words doesn't mean the relationship ends. When you take the time to repair, you send the message that you love your child no matter what, including during these negative and sometimes very hard or disruptive moments. Children learn that even when mistakes are made and intense feelings are felt, repairs and reconnection are still possible. This knowledge anchors them and helps them grow their trust in you and your relationship. This communication is also an important part of helping children feel safe and grounded within themselves. It supports their learning to not be too hard on themselves for the mishaps that will happen. It is part of life, of relationships, of growth and learning together.

Meeting the essential need for safety enables your child or teen to develop and reinforce an internal sense of stability and trust, that they are okay and not alone, even when changes happen to or around them. During their growing years, they rely on us to reinforce that inner feeling of safety by showing them they can trust us. Each time we come back together with them and make the effort to reconnect genuinely, that trust is reinforced. In turn, they learn to trust themselves and know that they will be able to return to a sense of safety and being okay when any kind or degree of disruption or change happens, whether in our relationship with them or in their lives.

When some families were temporarily separated from one another because of COVID-19, I suggested family members stay connected virtually and be very clear to let the child know that "Soon, Daddy will be back, and we will have dinner together again." At the same time recognizing their feelings with reassurance matters: "You are worried about Daddy. You wish he were home. He will be okay." Children need to know that an absent parent or other family member is okay wherever they are, they will return, and routines will resume. For one separated family, the father was in a Latin American country visiting family when the world shutdown and the borders suddenly closed. It was frightening for everyone, and their six-year-old refused to go outside for several weeks, even for a short amount of time. This was a challenge in a small apartment. As soon as the dad got home, she started going out for a little time each day until she felt safe playing for extended periods, knowing that they were all back home.

During times of crisis, being our child's anchor and container can be difficult. In one example, a family was separated when one parent was working while the other parent took their two- and five-year-old children on a camping trip. During the trip, a wildfire broke out and the father and two children had to drive through a wall of fire to escape.

Stressed and trying to keep calm, the father kept his eyes on the road ahead and worked hard to maintain his composure. Understandably, he was frightened and had one goal: getting his family to safety. I asked him how he stayed calm through this terrifying ride. He noted that even though he was aware that they were in danger, he wanted to make his children feel safe, so he put on children's songs in the car, and they sang along. As his son noticed the colors of the flames, they began to sing songs about colors. The dad then suggested they sing songs about rain, wishing for rain to put out the fires. "The whole time, I just tried to stay calm as I looked ahead and focused on us getting out of the fire."

A week later, when I was in touch with the family again, the father was still quite shaken. He knew the danger they'd been in and was now experiencing nightmares. Although he sought emotional help for himself, his children were back in school and day care with no negative impact as far as he could tell. When I asked him how the children were doing, he told me that the children had talked about "singing in the car with Daddy."

It was clear to us both that the children had minimal awareness of the danger they were in due to the father's ability to buffer them from his own fear.

So how do we best help our children develop this internal sense that they are okay even in times of uncertainty or crisis? We want to help them know they are not alone and that we are there with them and to reassure them that they are safe and taken care of, even when we do not feel safe ourselves. They can carry this stable feeling with them, even if you are not physically close by. One way parents can do this is by reminding your children of previous times when you as a family got through something hard together. These explicit reminders anchor them in the moment and help build their reservoir of resilience, along with you acting as their buffer from stressors, as best as you can.

The You Factor

Staying grounded in the face of our children's meltdowns, rude behavior, or inability to listen to our requests is rarely easy. What can help us manage our own reactions is to remind ourselves that children are not mini-adults. Far from it. Neither are adolescents. I highlight this point because there will be times when our expectations for our children do not align with their capabilities at that moment. We may ask them to handle experiences they are not yet ready for, and their inability can take us by surprise. For example, perhaps you feel certain your child can handle being dropped off for a birthday party, trying a new sport, or speaking at a poetry jam, and when they refuse, or otherwise show you that they cannot do it, you get disappointed, flustered, even upset. Similarly, when our children get upset, we might first feel frustrated, especially if they don't calm down at our direction. We may get angry and take a step away, just when they need our support.

For example, one of my teenage children angrily marched into the kitchen one evening clearly upset and yelled a strongly worded and abrupt request at me, something like, "You said you were the one finishing the laundry tonight! And I don't see the pants I wanted! Why did you say you were doing the laundry when you weren't?! I would have done it myself!" He was fuming.

Should I have told him to change his attitude and punished him? Yell at him for speaking this way? Truth is, I was taken aback by his anger and tone at that moment, which felt like an attack. I am not a fan of being treated like that, and I had no idea what was driving it, although it was clear he was upset. I managed to take a deep breath and get my grounding (I often use mantras like "Don't take this personally. Be the adult") so I did not get defensive or lash out. I also tried to decouple the pieces at play: 1) he could be mad, but 2) he could not speak to me like that. I knew enough to not take my child's reactions to their emotions personally. I would not be able to help him regulate if I was busy being defensive, and yet I had to work to stay grounded.

I looked straight at him and calmly but firmly said, "You're angry, but I suggest you step out, come back, and try that request again . . . in a new way." I said this with a bit of humor to convey that I was not taking his behavior personally; but I also wanted him to know that I would not respond to this type of demand. I was setting a limit along with showing an openness to hearing about his need.

To my surprise and delight, I saw his shoulders relax, and then he turned and walked out. Within moments he came back with a slight smile and said, "Mom, I need my clothes. I can finish the laundry."

And with that, he ambled off to the laundry room. No shame, no blame, and later he came back and apologized (you never know when that will happen, but it does). He acknowledged that he had been upset about schoolwork and wanted his favorite pants and not finding them put him over the edge of frustration. We laughed about his first request and then the redo on the second.

The point here is that the lighter we can be in ourselves and the more aware of our own need for grounding, the more able we are to help our children learn to handle tense situations. In this example, I acknowledged my son's anger, but I also set my own boundary, which set the stage for the repair and reconnection. By exhaling and staying focused on my own reaction first, I was able to respond with a reasonable limit and not a punishment. He was able to leave, regroup, and return with a lighter attitude and an apology. The mishap was behind us, we were positively connected again, and we could move on.

REFLECTIVE QUESTIONS

As you think about how best to infuse and reinforce a sense of safety in your relationship with your child, ask yourself:

- Are you aware of your children's basic needs? How do you go about trying to meet them?
- What gets in your way of seeing what your child needs?
- What family routines do you have in place to anchor daily schedules?
- How do you respond when your child is upset when a routine gets changed?

- How do you tune in to individual children amidst shifting circumstances?
- Who helped you feel safe when you were a child and needed support? What did that feel like?
- How might your own experiences be affecting or shaping your perspective of a situation and how you respond to your child?
- Are you aware of your own reactions during stressful moments? How do you address your own needs so you can be available to help your child?
- What might you do to understand your own reactions?
- When your child is distressed, how does that make you feel?

CHAPTER 4

The Balance Principle

Pillar Two: Learning to Regulate

Helping children manage the intensity of their emotional experience and understand the vast range of their feelings is the backbone of helping them learn to self-regulate, the process by which they gradually learn to adjust to changes, disappointments, losses, and any kind of interruption in their status quo. The faster or more easily a child can regain that internal balance, the more capable they become at handling stress, adjusting to it, and moving on. And when we help them build these regulation skills, children are better able to absorb stressors, deal with changing circumstances, and stay grounded and functional. You may think it's not good for your child or teen to be sad, upset, or angry, and that it's your job to protect them from such feelings. I am here to tell you that the opposite is true. Strong emotions—especially the negative ones—are not only natural but also necessary to becoming a well-adjusted person. Avoiding, dismissing, or burying these feelings will only cause pain by forcing their feelings to fester inside, halting your child's development and otherwise interfering with their personal growth. In contrast, when children learn to identify, feel, accept, and manage their feelings, they learn another crucial skill of resilience: how to self-regulate.

Attuned parents can teach their children to pay attention to their own brain-bodies, so they can become more connected to their internal arousal and the concomitant emotional experience. Parents do this quite naturally through their many interactions, especially when children are upset. With parents' help, again acting as the container for their children's emotional experience and an anchor of safety and consistency, children will be able to identify and process both positive and negative emotions without getting derailed by their intensity.

When children have a parent who allows them to experience the full range of their feelings without scolding or ridiculing them, they learn to accept their feelings instead of feeling ashamed of such emotions. It's our job to help them feel understood and supported so they, in turn, learn how to understand negative or difficult emotions and manage them even in uncertain times. Further, the understanding that parents show to their children—even when it's challenging—is the model for how their children learn to treat themselves and others. Children learn to extend empathy and compassion to others by first experiencing being understood and treated reasonably, kindly, and without judgment, especially in their hardest moments.

Keep in mind that there's great variability in how and at what rate these regulatory skills develop and get mastered; there's no one timeline or single way to grow or teach children how to manage their feelings and behavior. Additionally, children in the same family or household will differ in how they develop regulatory skills, which can further complicate your life as you focus on understanding each child's unique ways and reactions. And just when you think one child is getting better at it and you can step back a bit, another may show you they need more help and attention.

• • •

Co-Regulation: It Takes Two

Part of being your child's anchor and container involves you helping to co-regulate their brain-bodies. In an immediate way, a baby or young child relies on you to help them calm, soothe, and bring down their arousal. Consider the graph below:

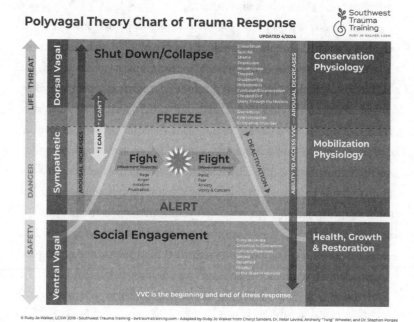

FIGURE 4.1

Stephen Porges's Polyvagal Theory of Arousal

Adapted by Ruby Jo Walker, Southwest Trauma Training, with permission

The high point is similar to a high temperature that reflects the rising arousal of the child's brain-body system. When the temperature rises above the one hundred level, for instance, you move into action to help the temperature (or fever) return to a neutral, more balanced state (non-fever). You do this quite naturally: when your child is distressed, you move closer to help soothe them or try to understand what is causing their upset. When we help bring down the temperature of their arousal, we allow their brain-body system to come back into a balanced state, which in turn engenders feelings of safety and equilibrium. Over time, helping the child (or teen) return to this balanced state after feeling intense emotions or simply feeling off-kilter, reinforces their inner sense of being grounded and their ability to trust themselves and others.

In contrast, without the presence of or support from a trusted adult, a child will have trouble regulating and feeling secure in themselves, which can show up in different ways: their sleep may be off, emotions get out of control, their behavior may be impulsive or reactive, or they may be withdrawn, quieter, and shut down, which can be harder to spot. These can be signs that they're having trouble regulating in these moments and lack an inner sense of safety that they so badly need. Typically, this action of parents or caregivers stepping in closer to assure a child they are okay is enough to lay down the foundation for a child to eventually mimic the process on their own. As children grow and teens face new and intense feelings, parents and other adults can also reinforce self-soothing techniques by introducing or modeling suggestions such as:

"I see you're upset; let's take a walk" or "Maybe a walk or going for a run will help you feel better."

"Let's sit down and read a book together. I am happy to hold you on my lap."

"Are you afraid of that doggy? I know it's a big dog, but I'm not going to let it harm you. We can walk a little closer together."

"This is really worrying you; I am here if you want to talk."

"You are so upset right now. Would writing in your journal be helpful?"

Paying attention to your child's unique rhythms, vulnerabilities, stress points, and needs will enable you to stay connected and anticipate what might cause them to become upset. Regardless of the cause (and no matter how ridiculous you think the cause may be), it's your child's felt experience that you are cuing into and you must suspend your judgment of them, though that's not always easy to do. Some of the calming takes place physically in holding a child, giving them a hug, or putting a gentle hand on their shoulder or back. Other soothing can happen through your communication. Try to be a good listener, offering words or gestures of understanding and empathy. Being an attentive, calm listener can go a long way in helping your child feel better, and it is a skill we often underestimate in terms of being present for them.

So what do you do when the meltdown, upset, or tantrum is at a very high level? At times of high emotion, your instant reaction to the intensity may be to tell your child to "just calm down, cool it." High emotions can move us to become more controlling. The problem with such a top-down direction is that it's rarely successful. I get it: as a parent you are upset; and yet if you can get yourself to take a step back and see the bigger picture, you will likely realize that these quick reactions mostly backfire. The child feels the parents' tension or aggravation, which can make your child get even more upset. In these heated moments when your child is already overwhelmed by emotions, giving them directions or commands won't work; shouting "Calm down!" "Stop crying!" or "Don't worry about that!" will likely not be heard by your child and can instead escalate the already intense situation.

The first step in helping a child in distress is to connect to them, whether they fell on the playground and got hurt, or if after a rough day in middle school they came home in tears. In this emotionally elevated moment, your child needs you, the parent, to step back and return to the grounded parent place to help them. Awareness of what your child needs can radically alter your approach. The key here is remembering that 1) your connected relationship is what matters; and 2) the goal is to help your child regain grounding, so they can return to being calm and balanced.

Each time a parent helps co-regulate (calm) their child, the child gains practice. It takes a lot of practice with experiencing their arousal going up-up-up (upset) and back down (steady, more grounded again) before children can manage it on their own. Their brain and body absorb and encode each episode of co-regulation as part of learning to handle their emotions. For example, when four-year-old Xavier hears that there are no more Cheerios, he bursts out screaming and throws himself to the floor. Sofia, his well-meaning parent, tries to explain that she will buy him more later, but the emotions have overtaken him, and no reasoning can help right now. When sharing this story with me, Sofia reported that Xavier "knew we would get more at the grocery store later," which left her perplexed as to why he threw such a big fit.

I pointed out that while it was true that he probably did know about a plan or promise to get more Cheerios later, he was not able to be aware of that during his outburst. His emotions were flooding his brain, and for those moments of emotional meltdown, any rational thinking is nearly impossible. As children get older, their rational abilities grow stronger as they become better able to withstand the emotional outbursts, but for Xavier, in the heat of that moment, the emotion and cognitive pieces are inextricable. When emotions are heightened, it can be hard for any of us to stay focused, let alone reasonable or rational, in our thinking. The challenge as a parent is keeping our own emotions in check, so that we can focus on helping our children learn to calm themselves when upset.

In another example, a frustrated fifth grader becomes almost apoplectic because she cannot figure out how to build a complicated structure as part of an ongoing school project on building bridges. Typically, she is a confident problem-solver, but once upset, she easily loses her ability to think through possible solutions. Emotions can overpower a child's thinking or cognitive capacities at such moments. So how best to help a child or teen move out of this highly dysregulated state and calm their overwhelmed system? At this initial stage, it's about helping your child reestablish their inner equilibrium.

Based on the work and conversations with my colleague and Duke University graduate schoolmate, Laura Bennett Murphy, a highly regarded pediatric psychologist and trauma therapist at the University of Utah, I have adapted the work she does with severely traumatized children for use in more generalized, but emotionally charged times. The techniques are found throughout this chapter. This first exercise has to do with the child's biophysiology and helps them move from dysregulation to a calmer, steadier place by bringing down arousal. Try to keep your focus on that singular goal:

1. Start with a focus on grounding yourself.
   i. Feel your feet on the ground, firmly planted.
   ii. Visualize the hard floor or ground and ask yourself, "Are my feet on the ground? Am I steady?"
   iii. Exhale, then slowly inhale deeply to steady yourself and bring down your arousal. Repeat 1–3 times until you feel your breathing become regular.
   iv. Remind yourself that your child is doing the best they can and mindfully separate your child from their behavior. Do your best not to take their actions personally.
   v. Use a mantra to reinforce your awareness:
      • "I am the grown-up."
      • "I can handle this."
      • "They need me now."

vi. Take another slow breath and remind yourself that this current and huge upset is just one moment in time. Whatever is happening within your child will not last forever and is not a reflection of how they behave or react to all situations; this is one day or night, and the two of you can get through it. If you begin to feel stuck or overwhelmed, remind yourself that you can handle this moment; you have done it before. Think about a positive outcome from the past as your reminder.

Once you have returned to more grounded equilibrium yourself, you can turn to helping your child. An aroused, dysregulated parent is not one who can help a child bring down their arousal.

2. Turn to helping your distressed and dysregulated child.

i. Help your child breathe more slowly as a starting point to calm their system. Try taking a slow, deep breath yourself and exhale audibly at a slow pace (a hum can work), so your child hears you and feels your supportive presence and slowed breathing. You can try encouraging them with gentle words: "Take a slow breath, you're okay, breathe slowly, I am here." Breathing practice is about helping your child establish a rhythm. It works for some children, but not all. Don't worry if it does not work every time for your child but know that your calmer breathing will still be felt by them.

ii. Look at your child with care, touch or hold them, if they will let you. You want them to feel your connection, to know you are there with them, however they can receive that in the midst of their upset.

iii. Now you can begin to reorient them to the present and what is going on:
- Narrate the moment. Calmly describe to them what is happening; put words to it and make a connection to the child's experience. Your child will begin to respond to the grounded nature of the parent. For example:
  » "You fell off the climber and that hurt a lot."
  » "Your friend did not respond to your texts and that upset you."
  » "The big test was not what you expected and that was a huge disappointment."
  » "You thought I should do that for you, and when I did not, it really made you mad."

iv. Remind your child you are there for them: "We can handle this together"; "This is hard, and it will pass; we'll get through it"; "I am here; I will help you."

v. Avoid any shaming or blame for their behaviors or how they feel.

We all need ways to self-soothe and handle intense emotion. It is human to get upset. We all want to be able to soothe ourselves and feel calmer. As children grow, you can steadily and over time pull back while they learn to handle these moments more on their own, continuing to remain nearby for support and help as needed. Eventually, the child's ability to handle intense emotions or disruptive moments gets better (a relief for the parent!), and they become more and more capable of calming or soothing themselves mostly on their own. Some children will take longer to learn these soothing and regulating skills, and even the child who handles emotional upheavals well one moment and has created reliable coping mechanisms cannot do so all the time. Your help is still needed.

Having a set of techniques to address a highly upset child or teen is helpful, and it's best to have more than one strategy to try. At a moment of intense emotions, you may need to try different ways to first connect and then bring down the situation. Just because one attempt fails does not mean you have done something wrong. It can take a few different attempts to figure out what works for your child generally, or in any one unique moment.

Using the Senses to Help Calm Your Child

I begin here with techniques for helping calm an upset child that uses the five senses to bring down the child's physiological arousal. Engaging their physical senses (touch, movement, sound, squeezes—depending on what your child responds to) can reorient them back to the here and now and to re-regulate. When a child is highly upset, they can lose their sense of where they are and what is happening to them. Connecting to them physically can be soothing. You will have to try different approaches to see what works for your child, knowing that their response may vary at different times. A few ways to do this (and try on your own, too) include:

- Squeeze something soft. Playing with play dough or a squeezable toy can release pressure. Squeezing hands into fists and releasing (guided by a parent) can also help; or try having your child grip your finger hard, hard, harder, then release.
- Ask them to tense their toes and release; repeat this three to four times. Do this with hands and fingers. You can model it as you say the words.
- Raise shoulders and release. Lift and let go of the shoulders.
- Massage their hands, fingers, or feet with gentle pressure. You can say the connecting words, "I've got you. I'm here with you. We've got this," while you do this.

- Hug or hold your child, with firm squeezes of the elbows, arms, shoulders, or thighs.
- Turn on music. Listen to soothing music or, for some, music that lets them rev up, move a lot, and then calm down as it gets slower. Try music that goes fast and then slow.
- Get in motion. Ride a scooter, run in the backyard, jump on a trampoline, jump rope, sway back and forth with your child (either near them or, if younger, holding them), slowly walk together.
- Spin tops. Spinning a top and watching it go around calms children of all ages.
- Make sounds. Humming can be calming. With your child, take a deep breath and hum out as long as you can; then inhale slowly and deeply, repeatedly. They can hear you and may start to join in on the humming.
- Use a cold compress. To counter the extreme emotion and upset in a heated situation, lay a cold compress, a wet washcloth, or an ice pack on their forehead, back of neck, or wrists to bring down their physiological temperature. Make sure to narrate what you are doing and why: "I will place this on your neck to cool you." For older ones, a cool gel eye mask can be offered (even shop for one together to give them the agency in handling their emotions next time). Teens can splash cold water on their face or take a cold shower.

Another way to help your highly distressed child involves using the immediate environment to help them reorient to the here and now to help bring down their distress. This again involves using their five senses and ties into their physiological state, but be sure not to focus at this time on what led to their being upset, which may compound their agitation. Instead, sit with them as a support and gently guide them by reorienting them to their surroundings:

5. **Seeing:** Help them visualize and observe what's around them. You might prompt them: "Tell me **five things** you see in the room/close by." Ask your child to name what they see. If they are too upset, start with, "I see a [name an object]. Can you see it too?" (Alternatives to try: "Tell me five red things you see" or "Tell me five round things.")

Then proceed through the other senses with a countdown:

4. **Hearing:** "Tell me **four things** you can hear right now; one is my voice, what else?"
3. **Touch:** "What are **three things** you can touch or you feel right now?" You can start this exercise by prompting, "I feel the wind blowing on my face, the arms of the couch," and so on.
2. **Smell:** Guide your child to breathe in through their nose, prompting, "What are **two things** you can smell?" If they need more support, again, prompt them by describing what you smell.
1. **Taste:** Giving your child a bite of food or piece of candy, ask them, "What is **one thing** you can taste right now?"

This exercise helps lessen a child's aroused state and brings them back to the present moment. By going through the five senses together, you remind them that you are present to contain and anchor them, and they are not alone in this moment of emotional upheaval.

Distraction Can Help Defuse Intense Emotion

Addressing intense distress sometimes involves moving away from the situation, changing places, or finding a distraction so you can move your child out of an escalating spiral of emotions. Try these activities to help teach your child how they can regain their equilibrium and calm their brain-bodies; suggest they:

- Go for a walk together; there is no need to talk unless your child wants to.
- Take time alone in their room, the backyard, or in a quiet part of the house or apartment; this shows your child that being alone can be comforting (and not a punishment).
- Create a small hiding place where the world is more compact; make a fort with pillows or a tent under a table with a cloth hanging over it. If they want to stay close to you, perhaps you snuggle in bed or on the sofa.
- Stroke their pet or a favorite stuffed animal toy.
- Shoot baskets, throw a ball, or play catch with you.
- Climb a tree, go for a run, or do some other physical activity to bring down stress.
- Sit in nature, touch the grass, walk through a garden, take in the visuals and the smells, and feel the air or breeze.
- Sit with you and doodle or color side by side or on your lap.
- Read a book with you, or help them find a quiet place to sit and read themselves.
- Watch a movie or funny videos with you; look at calming nature videos or another calming genre your child enjoys.
- Write down their thoughts and feelings in a journal or notebook.

These are suggestions and do not have to be followed exactly. It is not about perfection, nor will you get it right each time. When one of these options does not work, you have not failed. It can take several tries; trial and error is part of figuring out what works for your child in that particular moment.

Teaching Emotions

An important first step in helping children learn to self-regulate is to teach them about their own emotions. Their brain wiring is very much in developmental flux (at times a lot of flux!) and a long way from being fully set; the ability to handle emotions and other skills of regulation (e.g., sustaining attention and focus and impulse control) takes time to fully form—up through their midtwenties and not before. The prefrontal cortex, the area of the brain that helps with managing emotions, is slowest to develop, which means they need your help more than you may think and often at times when you least expect it.

Yet it's not always easy or intuitive to label our emotions. Why? Because emotions are complicated, they reside within us, and they are abstract—we don't see them or physically touch them. We also tend to separate feelings into binary categories—happy or sad; angry or excited; anxious or calm; fearful or brave; lonely or connected; comfortable or uncomfortable. But in reality, emotions are rarely one thing.

I recall years back when I was trying to get pregnant, with some difficulty. I had just miscarried and was struggling to get pregnant again. Several of my closest friends were pregnant with their first or second children just as I was still trying to become a mother. When I would hear their news, I found myself flooded with a mix of feelings: happy for them, sad for myself, jealous, angry that I could not be pregnant (yet). It was a big realization for me, well into adulthood, of how complicated any one emotional reaction could be.

So how do we help our children gain understanding of something so crucial and yet so hard to grasp? As you likely did when they were still babies in your arms, you label their emotions without even thinking about it; such utterances as "That made you so happy," "Are you sad and missing Mommy?," "It seems like something is upsetting you." We do this in order to help children begin to understand what that unknown sensation is inside of them. A core component of the toddler program I run is labeling emotions for the children. What I see over time is children showing increased understanding of what they are feeling and increasing ability to express this in words. It is a process that takes time and repeated effort.

I observe toddlers every day as they suddenly stop what they are doing, look around, and then show an awareness of being frustrated (a furrowed brow, for instance) and begin to put two and two together about what they are feeling. Perhaps a toy was taken from them by another child, or they did not want Mommy or Daddy to leave at drop-off. They just now realize that the parent is gone, even though the parent said goodbye earlier. They may stomp their feet or utter words that express their anger. They need continued adult help to fully grasp what is happening, which we do when we narrate or label their emotions. As they gain more words for these unseen (but strongly felt) feelings, they feel (and act) with increasingly more self-assurance. Knowing our emotions is anchoring.

When we use words to describe emotions, adults also convey the sense that we accept whatever the child is feeling, whether they are upset, angry, disappointed, frustrated, scared, or any other feeling. This is important for the child to know, that they are still okay, even when they are upset, and that we are still there for them, as negative emotions can be worrisome.

So how can you help your child label and understand their emotions?

1. Start by labeling the feelings as you witness them:
   - "You look so excited! I can see it in your big smile."
   - "Wow, that girl is crying and stomping her feet. She must be so mad and upset."
   - "I see you are angry. I think that is why you threw yourself on the ground at the park."

- You can also describe your own feelings. "I was so frustrated today when I got to work and could not find my keys! I looked everywhere. But then I remembered that my friend at work had keys to my office, and she helped. I felt so much better."

  The meta message here is that it's okay to have these emotions, and that you, as the parent, can handle all their feelings. You are also signaling a general message that having negative feelings is a part of life: "Everyone gets mad at times!"

2. Make it playful and part of everyday interactions:

   - A simple song about feelings, starting when children are young—"I love you when you're: happy; sad; hungry; mad; yelling, etc."—can be shared with your child. Sing together or to them, and your child can add new feelings to the song as they learn them, too.

   - A fun mealtime ritual around how everyone is feeling helps children tie situations to their feelings. "Who has something funny that happened today? Surprising? Exciting? Maddening? Upsetting?" Make no obligation to answer, but the lighter and more fun it is, the more open children are to responding.

   - Practice making feeling faces with a child or picking out an emoji (Figure 4.2). Looking in a mirror together and sharing "feeling faces" can be a fun game that helps a child feel comfortable about having different emotions. You can do it first: make a frowning face, or mad face. Have your child copy yours, introduce their own, or guess what emotion each of you is showing.

3. Make emotions more tangible and real for children with the words you use and feedback you give them. Often, children and even adults have limited understanding of what and how

HOW DO YOU FEEL?

happy	confused	anxious	embarrassed	angry
content	frustrated	annoyed	scared	excited
sad	sick	disappointed	silly	confident
stressed	tired	loved	surprised	guilty
funny	worried	insecure	lonely	hurt

FIGURE 4.2

Name your emotions using emojis. Use this chart to help younger children learn to identify their feelings with more ease, picking a few at a time.

Used by permission of Elizabeth Low

they feel when they are upset. Here are some phrases about emotions to remind children about the nature of emotions:

- "Feelings change."
- "Sometimes you're happy; sometimes you're sad."
- "It's okay to feel that way."
- "Being so upset doesn't feel good right now. Feel it for now; it will pass."
- "What is your feeling trying to tell you?"
- "You can be sad/mad/upset right now; it won't be forever."

- "Everyone feels bad sometimes; it does not mean you are a bad person."
- "Everybody cries sometimes."

Consider these different emotions and how they connote varied nuances:

A List of Emotions

ANGRY	SAD	ANXIOUS
Grumpy	Disappointed	Afraid
Frustrated	Mournful	Stressed
Annoyed	Regretful	Vulnerable
Defensive	Depressed	Confused
Spiteful	Paralyzed	Bewildered
Impatient	Pessimistic	Skeptical
Disgusted	Tearful	Disgusted
Offended	Dismayed	Offended
Irritated	Disillusioned	Irritated

HURT	EMBARRASSED	HAPPY
Jealous	Isolated	Thankful
Betrayed	Self-conscious	Trusting
Isolated	Lonely	Comfortable
Shocked	Inferior	Content
Deprived	Guilty	Excited
Victimized	Ashamed	Relaxed
Aggrieved	Repugnant	Relieved
Tormented	Pathetic	Elated
Abandoned	Confused	Confident

FIGURE 4.3

Go beyond the obvious to identify exactly what you're feeling.

Source: Susan David

Feelings Are Embodied

It's also important to help children "sit in" or learn to stay with their feelings rather than feeling like they have to make them go away. We often want children to move on quickly from negative feelings, especially if we are uncomfortable experiencing those feelings ourself or letting them experience them. Conveying the message that it is okay to be sad means letting them be sad. "You miss Mommy; that's okay. Do you want to sit with me for a moment?" Once they have a name for an emotion as a first step, you can help them connect to the feeling as this is a somatic experience, where we feel the emotions within our bodies, just as much as it is emotional and cognitive.

Here's a brief exercise for how we can help children become more aware of and connected to their emotions:

1. Help your child become aware and name or label the feeling. Ask them what they are feeling, or name it for them.

2. Teach them how to get inside their body and allow the full feeling to be present (sit in the feeling). Suggest they close their eyes, pay attention to what they are feeling, and do a body scan, tuning in to where they feel this in their body. Help them to notice the sensations in their body, starting at the top of their head, down to the tips of their toes. You can guide them to try to locate that feeling in their body, such as a lump in their throat, butterflies or sinking feeling in their stomach, tightness in their chest.

3. Ask your child to note the feeling and the way it made them feel.

4. Return to the core reminder for your child that no matter what they are feeling or how badly it feels, you are here for them: "Even though you are (were) so sad, upset, angry, I still love you, I am here for you, always."

The feelings your child has are expressed in their behaviors, from being withdrawn and sullen to having aggressive outbursts and tantrums. Teaching children about their feelings also lays the groundwork for their learning which behaviors are socially acceptable, and which are not. When children experience negative feelings, some feel them quickly and act out physically. If a child throws a fork and you respond with "That is not something you can throw; if you want to throw something, here's a ball," you are teaching them what is acceptable to do and what is not. The same kind of redirection works for other behaviors that may stem from intense feelings, such as hitting and biting, which are also typical for toddlers and for some children beyond those years. While aggression tends to get less overt as children get older, it can be present at times of stress across ages. Regardless of age or developmental level, the idea is not to shame them for feeling negative emotions but to give a reasonable outlet to show them; this is what I call a reasonable limit. These negative behaviors are impulsive, meaning they happen quickly and without thinking in response to the emotion and the child needs help finding a way to better direct the impulse.

Providing clearly defined alternatives can help channel negative behaviors; for instance, as children need an outlet for the impulse, with a boundary:

"Here's a basket; throw that toy in here."
"Stomp your feet if you're so mad!"
"Biting your arm will hurt you; biting is for apples—let's get one."

The same will be true for older children or teens:

"I hear how upset you are about your friend; rather than kicking the furniture, you can go outside and kick a ball or shoot baskets."

"It's okay to feel angry, but it's not okay to throw your stuff all
over. Maybe writing in your diary will help you feel better."

As you redirect and acknowledge what they are feeling, try to incorporate lightness or humor, if that is appropriate at the time; the lighter and calmer you can keep a situation, the better for your child's emotion regulation. Again, it's up to you to handle your own reaction so you can help your child. Ask yourself if your child's outburst is truly a crisis or if you can relax into the situation a little, which will then help bring the child's emotion and arousal back down. Your being able to stay (reasonably) relaxed and calm will help them contain their own intense feelings.

In helping your child learn to handle all the feelings that underlie these behaviors, keep in mind that the goal is not to be rid of emotions entirely. Emotions are our allies, giving us information about ourselves, our world, and our relationships. The goal is to keep the emotions within a "tolerable window" or a range where we can accept and use them. There will be times in your child's life when emotions remain very present (especially grief or an ongoing social problem like divorce or friendship conflicts) and reflect the difficulty of a situation. Knowing we are not alone in those moments is key to making our emotions a source of resilience, not something to ignore, avoid, or deny.

Recognize and Help Manage Stressors

Another important role of the parent-child attachment relationship is helping children learn to manage the inevitable stressors they encounter in their daily lives and the accompanying emotions that go with them. By "stressor," I mean any disruption in a routine—from a sudden change to a child's environment to a physical illness; a stressor is any internal or external factor that pushes a child out of their equilibrium. Stress is not necessarily a bad thing: it's what tells our brain to pay attention, adapt, grow, and learn. Stress heightens our attention and can increase our focus. Before children learn to manage stress on their own, they once again rely on us to strengthen their stress response systems. This is the ultimate purpose of regulation.

As has been shown in numerous rodent and mammal studies, until three months of age, a child's stress response (as measured by cortisol—the stress hormone—levels) stays relatively low, which may seem odd since newborns would appear to be more vulnerable to outside stressors once out of the safety of the womb. You may think their stress hormones would start out higher. In fact, that is not the case. This "hyporesponsive period" suggests that the low levels of cortisol reflect the parent's presence and calming effect on the newborn's nervous system, allowing the newborn or rat pup a window to attach to a primary caregiver. The parent helps the child "modulate emotional arousal for adaptive functioning"—this is a fancy way to describe the process of—or skills related to—how we all learn to manage stress and regulate our emotions, particularly the negative and intense ones like anger, disappointment, and frustration.

One way I help parents understand the significance of this stress response is to bring to mind the biological concept of homeostasis. As one of the primary drivers of our biology, all human beings (and animals) are in a constant process of staying in a physiological state of balance. Balance feels good! This is happening without our even realizing it because it's run by the autonomic nervous system, a part of our brain that is always on and works below our conscious awareness. This drive for balance and grounding works in different ways to keep us safe and healthy. Any stress that we encounter—whether that is a lack of sleep, a very cold or extremely hot day, hunger or thirst, giving a public speech, receiving an upsetting phone call or email, the death of a pet—is the type of stressor that pushes our brain-body system out of balance. As researchers note, "Stress is now defined as a state of homeostasis being challenged, including both system stress and local stress."

As soon as we encounter a stressor, our brain-body makes quick decisions to send energy where it's most needed to bring the body back into homeostasis. The brain-body works in many ways to achieve this balance and regulate itself, including through the cardiovascular system, metabolism, respiratory system, temperature control, and osmotic balance (right level of fluids/salt for proper functioning of kidneys). Together, these systems work automatically without our ever thinking about it. Though this is an oversimplified way of explaining a highly complex regulatory system, it's helpful to keep in mind that the purpose of our stress response system is to help us adjust to the ever-changing environment in which we live and so that we don't live in a chronic state of high alert, vigilance, or anxiety, at least under normal everyday situations. Like other aspects of homeostasis, the stress response system is essentially a regulatory mechanism that ensures our safety, survival, and overall physical and emotional health and well-being. The more agile we are at calming down our brain-body after a stressful experience, the more adept we are at handling our emotions in general.

However, not all stress is bad for us; there's also the concept of good stress, which researchers refer to as "eustress." This type of lower-level stress is essential for our well-being because it helps the brain-body system practice responding to stress during smaller, less threatening moments. Think of this as similar to working out a muscle; gradually, with steady exercise and strengthening and without overtraining, the muscle gets stronger. "Short" exposures to stress can be beneficial, says NYU developmental neuroscientist Regina Sullivan, because stress provides our bodies with the ability to practice our responses. Stress can also be motivating, even exciting—that "good nervousness" that keeps you focused and awake, such as preparing to give a big talk or taking a test you feel well prepared for. The system for handling stress needs practice, and "good stress" allows for that.

Picture the toddler who hasn't eaten much in days because of a bad cold and when she arrives at Grandma's new, unfamiliar apartment she breaks down in tears (even though she loves seeing Grandma).

Think about an overtired child who can't calm down no matter how much comfort you're offering but keeps insisting, "Don't leave me alone!"

Consider the stressed-out student who, facing a big exam, hasn't slept more than five hours a night for over a week and has eaten only junk food. The day before the exam, he is so sensitive that any comment is heard as criticism, and he reacts defensively no matter what you say.

Lack of sleep, food, and drink will push the body out of balance, as will breaks in routine—especially for younger children—and often these physical stressors have emotional repercussions and cause breakdowns. These examples show how environmental stressors impact equilibrium, throwing us off-balance; being off-balance throws our emotions off, too.

Well beyond the sensitive period of infancy when the initial wiring is being set primarily through the loving care of the parent-child attachment relationship, children continue to grow and develop in the context of their environment. This not only includes their physical surroundings—home, school, access to food, safety of the neighborhood—but goes deeper than that. Environment also encompasses the relationships, the routines and rhythms of the day, and the reactions they and others have to their negative and challenging moments.

When stressors occur in the environment, whether that is momentary, recurring, or chronic, these environmental and relational elements take on an elevated importance. For example, living with financial hardships or in a household that is in upheaval will add stressors to a child's life, and yet a loving relationship with care and support can act as a buffer to help protect against some of the negative impacts. The point is that an environment in which a child lives plays a substantial role in how they develop the capacity to regulate and manage stress; what constitutes their environment involves multiple pieces, and at the center is their relationship with you.

Each of us—adults and children—is guaranteed to encounter stressors in our daily lives. Stressors can be small or big, inconsequential or major. Either way, in the moment, stressors destabilize the child as well as us. Teaching children that they have the capacity to deal with such stressors will lead them to internalize a sense of agency and give them feelings of control over their own experience, a core building block of resilience. An important first step in helping your child become resilient to stresses they encounter is teaching them how to first recognize the source of stress.

What can set your child off? There are many aspects of a given day that can act as stressors that upset your child or cause them to act out. These can include:

Everyday Stressors
- Clothes they want to wear are in the laundry
- Feeling hungry
- Poor night of sleep; feeling tired
- Missing a parent who is away
- Falling down or getting hurt
- Missing the bus for school
- Being late for school, or a sports or musical practice
- An upcoming exam or final presentation
- Leaving home each day for school
- Being unsure of a school assignment

- Starting a new school/camp/after-school job
- Teacher being out for the day; having a new teacher
- Having a fight with a sibling or friend
- Being picked last for a game at recess

Bigger Stressors

- Moving to a new house or city
- Moving to a new school
- Trying out for a sports team, orchestra, or community play
- Birth of a new sibling
- Separation or divorce
- Peer rejection/bullying
- Overscheduled/too much going on
- Ongoing school struggles or failure
- Accidents and serious injuries
- ER visits
- Illness of the child
- Illness of an adult
- Death of a relative
- Death of a pet

Chronic and Potentially Traumatic Stressors

- Financial hardships and losses
- Living in poverty, financially stressed, or in unstable circumstances
- Death of a parent or loved one
- Hunger or food insufficiency
- Lack of access to medical care or medications
- Emotional, verbal, physical, or sexual abuse
- Domestic violence

- Community violence
- Prolonged parental absence (illness, jail, divorce)
- Major disruption or relocation from natural disasters/climate emergencies or political violence or war
- Severe accidents
- Severe or chronic illness; hospitalizations

While we often view young children as being more carefree than adults, we underestimate the many stressful moments that even the youngest children witness or encounter. It is in these moments that a window of opportunity opens for children's learning. Look for these stressful moments and embrace them. We can chuckle about three-year-old Will screaming because his sandwich was cut "wrong" (he wanted it in half and his dad cut it in quarters—oh no!), but this is a real stress for that child when his ideas about the forthcoming lunch are not realized. A tragedy? No. Stressful for the child? Yes. And when Will's dad commiserates, notes how he made a mistake, and assures him that next time he will cut it "right," Will can eventually settle down and contain the emotional outburst.

When Zendaya comes home from school up in arms about a conflict with a close friend and the parent manages not to blame the friend (who often instigates these conflicts), she can identify her daughter's upset feelings, listen to her vent, and then, if Zendaya seems open to it, offer to come up with strategies for interacting with this friend that Zendaya can try.

Letting children and teens vent about all that went wrong today, especially after a long day at school, gives them the chance to unload all the stress or mishaps of the day. Listening without judgment or even feedback is often what they need—a sort of post-school-day unwinding with their most trusted person. This allows your child or teen to regroup and feel grounded again. They may go from fiercely venting and complaining to happiness a moment later; dumping out the bad parts can free up the rest. At times you will have to pull yourself back from giving advice or problem-solving and keep yourself in listening mode. But if you can do this, your children will talk even more to you. We don't always realize that being a trusted listener is what our child wants most.

The transition home from school after a full day is stressful for many children. Here's an example of eight-year-old Sadie, who was pushing her mother over the edge because she never had anything good to say when her mom picked her up. Her mother, Tatiana, complained that meeting her at the after-school program was like a volcano erupting.

"All she can do is complain about the teachers, about recess, about homework, you name it! You would think there was no good in her life."

I suggested that instead of expecting happiness at pickup after a long day, that she give permission for Sadie to have ten minutes of complaint time because she needed to let go of the stress of the day. I also encouraged Tatiana to be respectful but not take her daughter's words so seriously; no, her life was not terrible, but she needed to complain. "Tell her you want to hear all about everything, including the bad parts of her day," I suggested.

With this change, Sadie now had complaining time on the walks home, and she relished it. She was dramatic in her expressions of all that went badly that day. It sounded like she had nothing but bad stuff all day, which her mother knew was not true. But after dumping out all the bad for a bit, she would be done and stop. The two would reconnect. After a few days of this new tell-all routine that let her focus on the bad parts of her day, Sadie started asking her mom, "Did you have a good day today?"

This spontaneous turning toward her mother resulted from being listened to and feeling heard as her full self, even the negative parts, and from Tatiana no longer being irritated by the after-school venting sessions.

Moments like this capture the essence of how a child learns to handle their emotions and is part of a process of learning to regulate these intensely felt inner states. As children get older, parents can guide them on reflecting back on their experiences as a way to help them know their own growing regulation process. "Remember the last time you were upset about what your friend did? You came up with a plan to speak with her and the next day you were able to work together in math class." Reminders like these provide confidence since they can recall how they got through a similar situation another time. Your child learns both how to handle their own responses going forward and how to treat others—with respect and care. When you model that, in time they do it, too.

We can all bring to mind a myriad of ways that children's behaviors test our patience, and yet it's the emotional tenor and context underlying their behavior that is important to recognize. These, more than the behavior itself, are what drive our reactions—whether we perceive our child as rude and disrespectful, upset "for no reason," or overreacting to what we consider a small situation. Indeed, emotions are powerful fuel for all sorts of behavior—good and bad. Helping children become aware of the vast range of their feelings is the backbone of helping them learn to self-regulate, the process by which they gradually learn to understand and then manage their emotions as well as adjust to changes, disappointments, losses, and any kind of interruption in their status quo (e.g., their equilibrium). Again, when their equilibrium is out of balance, regaining stability is what fosters feeling safe again. It is from a place of safety that any of us can be our best selves. So, the faster or more easily a child can regain that internal balance, the more efficient their self-regulatory skills become and the better they are at handling emotions.

At the heart of helping our children learn to self-regulate is teaching them that emotions are not wrong or bad; emotions are information about how we are responding to a situation or person in our environment. When children learn to name and sit with their feelings, all feelings, regardless of how negative they are, they take a HUGE step in learning how to adjust and manage themselves in the world.

The You Factor

Helping our children and helping ourselves go together. As I mentioned, we are hardwired to deal with stress and to protect our children from it. Of course, as their anchor and container, we need to be aware of our own tension and emotional arousal states, as those are what our child absorbs, feels, and, ultimately, responds to. So when our own body tightens, shoulders tense up, heart beats faster, our talking gets faster and louder, and our emotions gain intensity with anxiety shooting upward, it becomes more challenging for us to help calm or co-regulate an upset child, let alone a teen. At times of high stress, our primary aim is to bring down the arousal—first ours, followed by our child's. And it goes without saying that the better you know yourself and have techniques for handling your own worry, anger, frustration, irritation, and anxiety, the better you will be as your child's support, emotion teacher, and buffer.

At the same time, knowing your children will also help you better understand your own responses and reactions to each of them. I urge you to be honest with yourself and not be ashamed of how you feel or react to your child in these moments, but to use this information to shift to a more positive connection, which we all want as parents. The better you know and understand who your child is (which you won't get right all the time), the more able you are to help them grow and gain the skills to handle life. It's equally important to keep in mind that regulation itself is an ongoing, dynamic growth process in which children as well as adults will continue to develop as they gain experience in life, interact with peers and other adults, and encounter changes and stressors in their environment. The good news is that you, the parent, have a unique opportunity to guide children in this process of emotion regulation so that emotions don't have to get in the way, or at least not too often.

When I meet with parents, I put my arms out wide in a circle to motion that early in life the parent is the one enveloping the young child, containing them in order to teach them how to regulate. Then, as the child matures and begins to gain skills for regulating themselves, the parent gradually opens their arms and guides the process from more of a distance, slowly stepping back. The goal here is to be in relationship with our children in grounded and anchoring ways throughout their lives. It is not a perfect or exact way of being, and your relationship style will be unique to you and your child. Ultimately, when children learn to regulate their emotional experiences, they also learn to handle their behaviors due to increased self-awareness and agency.

As adults, we react—at times strongly and negatively—to our children's heightened arousal states. Try not to be hard on yourself when you do; we are all human and emotions drive our connections. Intense negative emotions are rattling. It can be challenging to respond in a steady way to a highly charged child or teenager, just when they need us to stay steady. This is our own challenge to find a way to do so; it takes reflection on why we react as we do, and practice.

One technique I suggest to parents is using mantras to keep yourself grounded. They worked for me as I raised three children, each one temperamentally different from the other and each having their unique way. These are phrases that quickly come to mind and remind you that "I am the adult," and "I can handle this." They help keep you grounded, may lighten up the situation for you (or even bring some humor to play), and allow you to engage with your upset child in healthier, more steady ways, letting you be their container, the one who can hold their very intense emotions. This not only helps you be the container to calm your child, it also provides your child a role model of how to treat people. Your child experiences your ability to stay (mostly) calm with them, even at their most upset times, and they learn to be this way with others, too.

Below are mantras that I recommend, but I encourage you to come up with phrases that work for YOU. Different mantras will be better depending on which child you are responding to and how you are feeling at the time:

> "She's just a little girl." / "He is still so small."
> "They won't be little forever."
> "This, too, shall pass."
> "I am the adult in the room. Be the adult."
> "He's not out to get me; he's just upset."
> "She means no harm."
> "I cannot take this personally."
> "Believe it or not, he needs me."
> "She's doing the best she can."

REFLECTIVE QUESTIONS

What is it that gets in the way of our staying calm in these moments of emotional upheaval? It has to do with what we bring from our past into being a parent. In order to help your child learn how to calm down and come back into emotional balance, it's imperative for you to be aware of your own stressors, emotional triggers, and ways of coping when upset.

The more you understand about yourself—a process that takes time—the better you become at helping your child. Here are some questions you can ask yourself to better understand your own reactions. Over time, this increased awareness can help you respond differently to your child.

- What does it feel like to allow your child to be upset? What comes to mind?
- Does your body tense when your child gets upset? If so, where does the tension take place?
- When does this typically occur?
- Do you ever blame someone else, such as your partner, your spouse, or your own parent, when something negative occurs?
- Who does your child remind you of when they are intensely upset or challenging you in some way?
- Think about your own parents' responses to you: Who comforted you when you were a child? Let you know that things would be okay?
- When you were a child, were you shamed or ridiculed for how you felt or acted? What did that feel like to you?
- Can you a recall a time you were upset and felt cared for in a positive way? What do you recall?
- Did you ever feel blamed when bad things happened? Were you told you that you were being bad? Yelled at or punished? Teased or belittled by parents or other adults?
- Do you wish something had been different when you got upset as a child? What do you wish your parents had done?

CHAPTER 5

The Freedom Trail

Pillar Three: Developing Agency

When children internalize a sense of safety and begin to self-regulate, they are primed to embark on another important developmental milestone: separation. Separation from parents enables a child to become their own person—to individuate, become increasingly independent, and develop an authentic sense of self, all of which are essential for them to develop agency. With agency comes motivation and an awareness of their own competencies, and these feelings of control over themselves and their lives are what fuel children's desires to explore the world around them, investigate their curiosities, and test themselves. Once again, their trust in your relationship acts as the foundation for all of this developmental work; when you continue to act as their anchor and container, you enable your child to separate in a healthy way and develop a sense of agency, the third pillar of resilience. Agency is a key element of resilience because it fosters self-reliance and motivation. A 2015 study out of Harvard titled *The Influence of Teaching Beyond Standardized Test Scores* identified agency as a key factor for children's motivation and success, more important than standardized test scores. The researchers defined agency as "the capacity and propensity to take purposeful initiative—the opposite of helplessness. Young people with high levels of agency [. . .] tend to seek meaning and act with purpose to achieve the conditions they desire in their own and others' lives." Agency is what propels children through life.

Parents who unwittingly hinder the separation process by not distinguishing between the child's seemingly opposing needs for autonomy and closeness undermine their child's ability to develop the agency necessary to make and learn from mistakes, to go out into the world and test themselves as separate people, and to relate to others on their own terms. Being able to successfully separate hinges on a child feeling safe enough in their primary relationships, knowing they can trust that you will remain their secure base and be available when needed, as they get ready to embark on a long and gradual journey to independence and becoming a resourceful, well-adjusted adult. Most children are intrinsically motivated to take steps to separate from the cocoon of safety parents provide, but stepping out from this enveloping comfort zone, even a little, is scary and confusing. This is why the separation process is neither linear nor straightforward; it happens over long stretches of childhood and in fits and starts. First, the child begins to push parents away and just as often pulls them close when they need a touchpoint or a moment of comfort or when they feel afraid or unsteady, which is what happens during times of uncertainty. The transition to school each fall brings up uncertainty, as does joining a travel sports team or a major storm that floods the basement of your house. Each time your child shows their independence—e.g., walking to the nearby store alone to pick up milk or bread, staying alone at home for an evening while you go out, riding a bike to a friend's house a few blocks away, creating a shopping list and baking a cake on their own for the first time—they may retreat back, asking you to sit with them at bedtime or acting out in nontypical ways. As much as children desire more freedom, they also need your presence. Two steps forward and a slide back is common in the journey to increased independence.

Let's go back to the image of the string between you and your child. Sometimes the string is held tightly by one or the other of you, and sometimes it is held looser, depending on your child's needs at any stage of development. The string's tension represents the bond between the two of you. It is always there, allowing you and your child to remain together on the journey of separation and independence over time.

Teenagers and young adults are still engaged in a related process of separation, though their signals are different: Your sixteen-year-old may yell loudly and vociferously for you to "Leave me alone!" or "Get out of my room!" Your returning college student may lash out with an "I don't need you; stop hovering." While these exclamations reflect their desire at that moment for autonomy and privacy, emerging adults also want you to be there, close enough, when they do need you, even if not right at the moment. In other words, the string gets longer and looser, representing both your trust in them and their growing ability to be on their own, but it's still there, connecting the two of you, with variations in tension reflecting your child's needs. No doubt, it can get confusing.

For parents, encouraging and supporting separation means establishing clear expectations, offering age-appropriate limits along with freedom and flexibility, avoiding controlling or overly protective behavior, giving reasonable consequences, and helping children practice executive function skills—those skills that underlie goal-directed behavior—all of which children experience within the container and anchor of their relationship with you. If this sounds complicated, it does not have to be. The stronger and more secure the relationship between child and parent, the firmer the foundation for the child to go out and discover the world.

Setting Expectations and Limits

Exploring their world includes trying out new tasks and experiences, taking risks, and making mistakes—vital aspects of children's learning about how the world works and how they move in it. It is part of getting to know themselves and where they fit in, what they like and don't. But in order to venture out at any age and take new steps forward (from starting preschool to going to their first high school social event), children need limits and boundaries to remind them that you are present or nearby to help if they do fall, falter, or fail. In the toddler years, these limits are explicit; young children depend on your telling them when to stop, whether that is on their scooter or throwing food or toys. Indeed, ages two to five is a period marked by testing out their level of control and seeing if you are serious about asserting limits— within the safe confines you provide. Giving children limits enables them to develop agency. When parents set reasonable limits at any age, children feel secure enough to take risks and try to figure out how things work on their own. Such limits might sound like this:

> "At dinnertime, we sit, we chat together, and we eat; no toys or
>   devices at the table."
> "You can throw a ball on the field, but not at another person."
> "You are upset, but that language is not okay; try asking
>   another way."

Your child and teen may act like they want to be fully in charge, but they feel safer and calmer when they move within the confines of reasonable rules set by a loving caregiver.

A large body of research looks into overall patterns of parenting that help children grow into responsible, successful adults. What we learn from this research tells us a lot about the importance of limits. The collective findings of decades of studies point to specific qualities in the parent-child relationship that best support children to learn about themselves and develop a sense of agency. These interactions involve setting reasonable limits in an approach labeled authoritative, first described in groundbreaking longitudinal studies by the research psychologist Diana Baumrind of UC Berkeley beginning in the 1970s. Studying a group of families and looking closely at their interactions over time along with the developmental outcomes of their children, she used the findings to identify a parenting style that is a combination of responsive and warm interactions and clearly defined structure, reasonable and age-appropriate limits, and clearly articulated expectations for the child. This parenting style has been researched and validated again and again across the globe and over thousands of studies in the past fifty years—and it's actually quite straightforward in what it entails. Authoritative style is rooted in parents being responsive and attuned so that they provide enough room for a child to develop autonomy, and it fits hand in hand with the concepts of developing a relationship that provides both container and anchor. This way of interacting encourages parents to connect with warmth and sensitivity while they continue to signal that they are in charge, not harshly but reasonably, and that they will safeguard the child and guide them, not rigidly but in line with their needs. This allows children to feel secure in their exploration. Years of research has shown that this parenting style helps children become:

- Confident and content with themselves
- Able to take responsibility and make sound decisions
- Strong at problem-solving and academic success through high school and college
- Trusting of themselves and aware of the needs of others
- Able to handle the ups and downs of emotions, which allows them to have strong social skills and relate well to peers

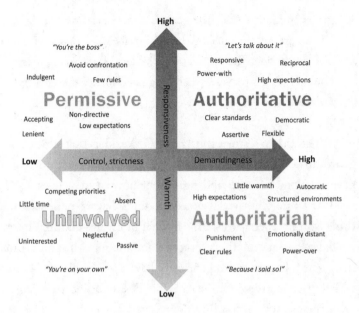

FIGURE 5.1

Sustaining Community

Used with permission by Graeme Stuart

Offering limits with freedom encourages children to explore, trust themselves, feel safe in the world from clear expectations, and be motivated to learn. I often think of a story that a colleague shared with me: Ildiko grew up in Eastern Europe under a dictatorship and was not raised with this balance of limits and freedom but instead with a much stricter authoritarian approach to behavior. She shared,

> When I was growing up, the adult would give a child a tricycle. They would draw a straight line and show the child how to pedal it straight from point A to point B as if there were only one way. And the child would have to do just that. They called it learning. But now I know that is not how to motivate children to learn or think. That only shows them point A to point B. Instead, you

give a child a tricycle. Then create a safe space, with hedges or a fence around the outside, the guardrails, a safe space with lots of room to ride. Then you let the child go. The child figures out how to ride the tricycle, where to go and makes their own path for riding.

What Ildiko's story illustrates is the idea that children need guardrails, to know where the boundary sits, but within that, they have freedom to move and figure out how to maneuver. Children need structure, but they also need room to have experiences and try things out for themselves. This is what motivates children to try out new ideas, create solutions, practice and master skills, and think for themselves. Creativity and curiosity have room to blossom—both of which drive learning. Curiosity is the desire to find things out, and joy is the pleasure of figuring them out.

Children also need to have a clear understanding of your expectations, which guide them in how to act in a variety of situations, along with your input and feedback. This feedback works best when it is not harsh or rigid but supportive. As you think about the kinds of limits and expectations you want to incorporate into your family, consider giving your children the room to think for themselves but with enough direction that they know the basics of what is expected. Keep these tips in mind:

- When setting a limit, use language that they can follow or understand. "It's time to do homework" is more clear than the question, "Do you want to do your homework?" Other examples include: "When you throw food, that means dinner is done; I see you are done." "I wish we could read more books, but we'll leave these here for tomorrow. Now it's time to say good night." You can be assertive and clear without being overbearing.

- Be explicit. Limits are rules of engagement. They are meant to communicate your guidelines for how to behave in a given situation. Children, regardless of their age, may not know what they are supposed to do, especially in new situations but also in repeated ones; taking the time to explain helps children understand different expectations for how to behave in various circumstances or contexts. "At the restaurant, we will have to wait awhile for the food, and you can sit and draw or play with your cars. We have to stay at the table." "When we get to the amusement park, you and your friend can go on your own onto the rides until 3:00. We will meet at the exit gates at 3:00, no later. And I will text you before if there is any change, so check your phone."

- Make sure that you've been understood. Does your child understand what's being asked of them? When the curfew is set for 11:00 p.m. for your fourteen-year-old to be home tonight, does she know that 11:00 is what you mean, that it is not 11:15, and that she is to wake you up to let you know she is back?

- If your child has trouble listening or following through on expectations, or seems set on pushing back on the limits, pause and reflect on what may be bothering, distracting, or frightening your child, or if they are seeking greater independence. Are they testing limits to figure out how much control they have? Are they in need of more time with you? Is there something going on with their friends, or are there stressors at school, like upcoming final papers? Are they asking for more responsibility and independence?

- Be flexible when you can. Offer limited options (the general rule of thumb is two): "I can pick you up at 5:00, or you can walk home with your brother a bit later." "Would you like to wear your sneakers or boots?" Children feel more motivated when they feel they have a say in the matter, which builds autonomy.

Setting limits and sticking by them is not always easy. Keep in mind two factors: 1) what you are trying to teach your child with any given limit or expectation, and 2) overall, that these collective guardrails help your child learn to organize themselves, which is an important step in learning how to regulate. At times we think that freedom translates to unlimited, open-ended possibilities. This is actually not the case. Unlimited possible options are overwhelming to children, and they are less likely to feel motivated or reach a goal when there are no constraints. It's also important to remind yourself that you are in charge, and being in charge means setting limits. Also remind yourself you've got this, even if your child pushes back.

For older children it can be helpful to discuss and agree on expectations together, which may include a type of written agreement that you develop together and refer to for navigating instances when agreed-upon rules are not followed or conflicts arise. Reaching these agreements may involve some healthy negotiation—which is good. Negotiation and compromise are life skills for your child, as long as you keep them within boundaries. (See chapter six for more about the role of healthy negotiations.) Engaging them in such discussions also shows your respect for their opinion, even when you don't agree. As you approach such discussions, think of them as conversations, not lectures. Lectures are not heard well by most people and also set up a pushback from the start given the top-down and one-way nature of a lecture. Instead, have some discussion where you are clear on your bottom line. For instance, you might say, "Walking home alone at that hour is not safe in my view; let's discuss the other options you have for returning home." At the same time, you are also genuinely listening and giving room for input.

I also recommend that you be as concrete as possible and succinctly explain your thinking, proactively clarifying possible consequences if the limits are not maintained. If the agreed-upon curfew is not followed, then follow through with your consequence. One of my children, who often pushed back on limits, commented to me while in high school:

> Mom, I figured out why you give me the freedom you do. We have trust. When you ask me to check in by midnight and tell you where I am, I do. When we agree upon a time for me to be home, even late times, I come home by then. But I realize that if I don't follow the rules we agree on, I'll be breaking your trust. You'd probably get stricter and make me come home earlier then. I get it now: it's not the actual curfew time that matters so much, it really is about trust.

He was right. Agreed-upon rules, curfews, and other limits with our children and teenagers are about trust, a key foundation of our relationship. Trust is also what is built, or broken, within the container of the relationship. After all, they will be moving out into the world on their own soon enough, so giving them the appropriate space and freedom enables them to become comfortable in the world, no matter how close by or how far away you may be.

Testing limits is quite normal for any age child and gets testier during certain ages; it can be healthy as children seek to figure out their boundaries and what they can and can't do in the world. Following limits rigidly is not the goal (which means you can let go at times; for example, pushing back bedtime when grandparents are visiting); it is better to aim for a goal of having your child develop general respect for the guardrails, meaning they follow most limits, have a sense of grounding and regulation within them, and push back or question them at times. So no matter how well-behaved your child is, how much you trust their judgment, how competent they may be in other areas of their life, they may still act out and test their limits (and I hope they do, as testing limits is part of building resilience). First, decide for yourself on which limits really matter to uphold and how much leeway your child has on other ones (i.e., where can you ease up?).

Six-year-old Lenox refused to hang up his coat on the coat hook when he got home, part of his responsibilities after school that had been clearly defined. He used to do it daily when he got home and put his shoes away, but now it had turned into a daily reminder and argument. Soon his father decided he would let go of it for the time being, as school was coming to a close and he knew that was a hard time of year for Lenox. Endings are uncertain, and children often get out of sorts. Regression is one way they show they are feeling unsteady. So his dad backed off. And sure enough, once school was over and they settled into the summer routine, Lenox, without being reminded, came into the house and put his coat on the hook and his shoes in the shoe bin. Simply reminding your children of your expectations can be enough; remind them, too, of any possible consequences that you laid out or agreed to (for example, "If you really cannot pitch in today with cleaning up the den with your sisters, then we will not be able to go on the hike later").

I find parents consistently have challenges when children do not like the limits and let the parents know. They rail against them, or sulk, or storm off as soon as they hear "no." Keep in mind that when you have reasonable limits, children are allowed to not like them, much less lovingly embrace them. It's more about clearly defining and articulating your expectations, including the message that you expect them to respect the rules and follow through. We all have to do things we don't like or want to do. As a parent, you have to be ready, at times, to keep to a limit you've set, even when your child is unhappy that you reminded them to make their bed, that playtime is over, or when you say no to going out on a school night.

For a time I had to pull a screaming four-year-old child of mine across major intersections because he did not want to hold my hand. My rule was that we had to be holding hands when crossing the city street, and they could let go on the other side. As soon as we reached the other side, I'd let go, and he would settle back down. Railing against that rule (although embarrassing as people watched me with this loudly screaming child) was something he could do. But holding my hand for that distance was not negotiable. The issue can be with you; parents take their children's negative reaction or pushback personally—even when the child abides by the limit but does so with protest—and get angry that their child is upset with them.

One mom said, "My daughter sulks as soon as I say it is time to put the electronic devices away. She is rude, looks down, stomps away."

I asked this mom what felt rude to her about the daughter following the limit while expressing that she did not like it.

"She has so much in her life. Why doesn't she just understand that she can't have it all the time and be okay with that? Why is she so mean to me?"

I understand; it is always easier when our children are agreeable. When children object or get mad at us over our limits, it can feel like they are spoiled. Another way to frame this behavior is as being part of separation, having their own opinions and reactions that separate them from us. In life we don't all agree, and out in the world they will not always like what they are asked to do.

I discussed with this mom what it means for her thirteen-year-old to become her own person, including the fact that her daughter might sometimes get angry with her parents and want distance. Trusting their parents means feeling able to show all their feelings, even the negative ones, which is at the heart of feeling safe enough to protest a limit. But just because a child pushes back or voices an opposing view doesn't mean we back off our limits. Just like the process of separation itself, developing a healthy dialogue around limits and consequences does not happen all at once. You will probably be returning to the so-called negotiating table throughout childhood and especially during adolescence and the teenage years and even into young adulthood—adult children do come home again and will need reminders of how to pitch in and respect your home. This process of understanding the reasons behind limits, your expectations of them, and possible consequences when trust is broken are all part of the larger picture of learning to be autonomous and responsible for their own behavior and actions. Limits and trust are related and support a child on the path to independence.

Push-Pull Across Ages

A child's drive to go out into the world and become their own person can clash with an equally powerful need for safety and to know they are not alone. We tend to think of separation related to young children, but they continue to struggle with their clashing needs for independence and safety well into young adulthood. When children begin to separate, they often do so with ambivalence—they want to be independent and do things for themselves, but also don't want to be too far away from you. And they don't want you to go too far, either. They are excited to get on the bus, but they don't like to say goodbye and get angry as they climb on; they don't want you to tell them what time to come home or to go to their room, but they want you to stay up late waiting for them, wanting to see the light on in your room when they return on a weekend night. Children are ready and not ready at the same time. Once again, without your presence and support, children will feel less steady and not so secure.

Attuning to small changes in behavior or moods will help you pick up on when your child may be having trouble separating and is in need of your presence that much more. Behaviors that signal separation may be difficult might look like:

- Your three-year-old who is waking up crying in the middle of the night
- Your five-year-old who wants to sleep in your bed
- Your seven-year-old who says about his best friend, "I don't want to go to Miko's birthday party!"
- Your ten-year-old who keeps getting tummy aches and doesn't want to go to school
- Your fifteen-year-old who insists on having you text them during the day, every day, to let them know you are okay

Perhaps you've given permission for your child to walk to school by themselves, assuming that this new freedom will be thrilling. But, surprisingly, your ten-year-old who has been asking to do this for months seems to be stalling at the breakfast table, can't find her other shoe, or sits in the bathroom for longer than usual. These are all indications that they may be afraid of leaving the house or your side, even though they crave freedom.

One parent told me that her highly independent and seemingly confident fourteen-year-old son said to her one morning, "Sometimes I wish I was in kindergarten again so you could walk me to school," even though he'd been going on his own and without hesitation, with friends, for years. Another child, age nine, had plans to sleep at her new friend's house. She sat on the couch with her backpack ready to go for the night, including the ingredients for cookies she wanted to bake for this special occasion. When her mother asked her to go tell her father they were leaving, she angrily barked, "Why do you always make me do things I don't want to do?!" Excited for the sleepover? Yes. Worried about separating? Also yes.

Separation is intense—even for the most ready and independent-minded of children. Here is an example of how separation worries can be expressed as children get older. Twelve-year-old Aleda could not fall asleep. She was starting a new after-school class the next day, a class she had been excited about for weeks. She had begged to take this class, where she would learn about writing her own graphic novel. The night before the first class, she laid out her clothes three times before getting in bed, switching outfits and unsure of what to wear for school the next day.

When her father, Rahim, came in to see if he could help her wind down, Aleda asked if he could pick her up the next day and let her skip the class. Her father recognized that his daughter's behavior was not typical for her—both the indecision of what to wear to school and her request to skip the class she had been eager to attend. He focused on these not-usual behaviors and thought about what was underlying them. This is what it means to be attuned; when Rahim cued in to Aleda's shift in mood and behavior, he proactively helped her to regulate. He realized that she was nervous about all the unknowns of the new class and brought up the possibility that she might be a little anxious about the class because it was new. After talking with her a bit, Rahim suggested Aleda attend once and then decide if she wanted to continue.

"Let's take this one step at a time," he explained. "I think you might enjoy it."

In the morning, Aleda approached the day a bit worried, but feeling more comfortable because of her father's suggestion that she could try one day.

In the end, Aleda enjoyed the class and wanted to continue. The support of her father got her through the fears of the newness and unknowns so that she was able to participate and take the class. She felt greatly empowered with her finished product at the end of the term, a fully written graphic novel. She also commented on how worried she was to start and how glad she was she still did it—this experience was clearly going to stick with her. Aleda experienced a sense of her own resilience when she was able to reflect on her initial worries and appreciate that she had gotten through the situation successfully. You may be able to recall a time when your child was starting something new—whether that was a first time sleeping at their grandparents, getting ready to attend summer camp, beginning high school, or doing their first school performance. Even before starting any of these activities, children will anticipate the event and wonder if they can handle it or be successful; anticipation can create worry about all the unknowns: "Will I have a friend?" "What if I forget my lines?" "What if I strike out each time I am up at bat?" As the anchoring parent, you provide the security by helping to narrate the situation with comments that let your child know you understand their predicament. For example, you might say, "I know you'll make a friend just like you did at the new after-school program, and I can't wait to hear about it," or "Remember, that everyone forgets lines sometimes; the theater director will be on the side to help you through."

The point here is that when facing a new or unknown situation, children will question their own readiness and brew self-doubts. Not knowing what to expect is steeped in uncertainties, which can make children feel fearful, hesitant, and less motivated to try something on their own. At these times, it's tempting for parents to step in and try to manage their emotions. With the best of intentions, parents can become overly protective and take away a prime opportunity for growth. When we as parents pause and keep in mind that these moments of separation, riddled with worries and ambivalence, provide opportunities for our children to test themselves and learn, we are helping them become more confident in their sense of agency, which is tied inextricably to resilience. When we encourage them while also supporting and acknowledging their feelings, they can discover their own strength and ability to handle difficult situations. Instead of pulling them out, we can help get them through.

Freedom to Make Mistakes

Children grow from their mistakes; it is an essential part of their learning process. In fact, younger children do not see mishaps as mistakes unless they are told it is wrong or that there is only one right way to do something. The renowned Swiss cognitive developmental psychologist and theorist Jean Piaget wrote about mistakes being important to children's learning as they use the information to adapt their thinking and incorporate new information to understanding how things work. Piaget referred to children as little scientists. If we stay on the sidelines and observe our little scientist, that young child will try many different ways to stack blocks high, reach an item on an upper shelf, or solve a puzzle, finding new strategies when one does not work. When a child says to themselves, "I want the tower to be higher, and when I put that one on, they fall, so now I will try a smaller one and see if the smaller one stays on," they are learning. This process of trial and error stokes creative thinking and problem-solving; it also supports a child's sense of their own agency.

How is this tied to separation? Separation means becoming one's own person. And becoming their own person means having their own thoughts, ideas, and desires to make decisions for themselves. I saw this type of thinking and learning firsthand on multiple visits to a unique set of schools in China called AnjiPlay and while speaking at their True Play conference. In AnjiPlay schools, preschoolers and kindergarteners are given broad latitude and freedom to play and learn in vast spaces with adults observing but not directing or interfering. What I witnessed were levels of collaboration, risk-taking, experimentation, and elaborate problem-solving beyond what I have ever watched in US settings. Children challenged themselves to learn when given space to play and own their learning.

For example, without set rules established by adults, children repeatedly built elaborate and large climbers or ramps for balls and tires to roll down. They next pushed themselves to complicate the apparatuses and test gravity by changing angles or sizes of what they rolled on the ramps. Mistakes? Plenty. They seemed to think of everything as problem-solving, exhilarating risk-taking, and hypothesis testing. When left to themselves, children eagerly came up with ideas and worked together with intensive negotiation, disagreement, and compromise as they decided how to improve what they were collaboratively working on. When we give children room to explore, try different ways to solve problems, and use their curiosity to motivate their learning, we free them from the dichotomy of thinking there is only one right way to do something.

As a parent, it can be hard to stay back and not run in and rescue our children when they flounder or fall. We want to remedy it so they are not frustrated or upset with themselves. Instead, we are likely taking away that opportunity for a child to pause and reflect on what they did, to come up with new ways of solving a dilemma, to be more creative about how they approach a task, or to simply decide to walk away and come back another time. Our rescuing them sends a strong message: we don't believe they can handle making a mistake or that making a mistake will hurt them and therefore is something to avoid entirely. If that is the message, we unwittingly undermine the resilience that comes from bouncing back after falling, after failing, or when things don't go as planned.

Learning is rarely straightforward. Sometimes children grasp a skill or task quickly, sometimes not. But each time they approach a task or try a new skill, children learn something—maybe they learn how to multiply complex numbers, or maybe they learn that they have to put in more effort. Maybe they learn in the first week of eighth-grade Spanish that they are having a lot of trouble following even the basics of the new language, or, conversely, that they have a quick ear for it. Maybe they come up with a new way to fit the animal pieces into the preschool puzzle frame, or maybe they switch and turn the wooden animal pieces into part of a toy farm. When we step in too quickly as our child struggles, we can inadvertently make our child feel insecure. Take your six-year-old on the playground who is left out of the play of other children nearby. You see him looking down at his feet, the children ignoring him. You worry: Will he ever approach children and make his way? Why aren't they inviting him in? Should I go ask for him? You could intervene, but watching and waiting may give him a chance on his own. To your surprise, he walks over to another lone child. Soon those two are playing together, and eventually they are playing with the bigger group. With time, and at his pace, he makes his way and runs back to tell you, "Daddy, I made a new friend!"

When we give them the space to figure out things for themselves or get back up after falling, we signal our trust and belief in our children. A common situation occurs at the Toddler Center when a child struggles to put on their jacket or Velcro a shoe. If I or any of the teachers step in and do the task for the child, the child won't learn to do it on their own. But holding a coat steady gives them a chance to zip it all the way up. I recall teaching one of my sons to tie his shoes. It was arduous and frustrating for him, and it would have been much faster for me to do it myself, and he probably would have preferred that, too. I could have taken over, but I forced myself to hold back (with a mantra reminder to myself—"Let him take his time; he's little") and wait. Eventually, he got it. The smile that ensued on his face was ear to ear. Though there can be many moments of failure and frustration along the way, children build confidence in their own agency and the resulting resilience that comes from reaching a goal.

If a child falls off a scooter or a bike, watch for a moment and see what they need: They may get back up on their own and ride off again, figuring it out. Or they may glance at you because they need help, or simply for a smile of reassurance. No need to rush in.

If a child comes home with a disappointing grade on a test, stop yourself from criticizing or making excuses for them; resist saying, "You were just tired on exam day, that's all." Instead, ask your child about the test, and be open to hearing what they have to say. Your supportive conversation conveys that learning is a process and it won't always go as well as they wish. Offer to go over the assignment, and if they agree, ask open-ended questions to help them become aware of either what they may not yet understand or what they could do differently.

If a child reports on a disagreement or conflict with a friend, even those that sound insurmountable to you, resist interfering or drawing a conclusion. Instead, ask your child to describe the situation, including their own role in it and feelings about it. Point out observations, ask questions, and try to listen to what your child has to say about their disappointment.

When children try again after making a mistake, they learn much more than simply how to do that task correctly. Whether they are trying to figure out a complex math problem, master a new physical skill, or learn how to read new vocabulary words, the struggle in itself is meaningful and often beneficial. It is not arriving at the answer that matters per se, but the realization that learning takes effort and time. This is what Stanford psychologist Carol Dweck refers to as growth mindset. There is currently debate about the efficacy of some of the prescriptive mindset interventions, but Dweck's main theory holds. Children who possess or develop a growth mindset believe that learning new skills, how to use materials, or how to approach novel situations takes time and effort; they believe that they can figure things out, that mistakes will happen along the way, and that success is always possible. Significantly, children with a growth mindset learn from their mistakes, believe they can keep growing their abilities, and don't think of setbacks as a sign of failure.

In contrast, children who exhibit a fixed mindset view mistakes or struggles as a sign of their failure and as something to avoid. This kind of thinking sets a child up to avoid challenges since challenges potentially lead to mistakes, and in their thinking, no good can come of that since it cannot be changed. They either know something or they don't, as if intelligence were given to them in a set amount and that is all they have. In reality, children are not all of one mindset or the other; they will have moments of each, depending on a variety of contextual factors, including the demands of the task, how they are feeling that day, attitudes they have about that subject area, and how well prepared they feel. But parents can help children cultivate a more constructive orientation toward learning by emphasizing the process itself, not its outcome; by focusing on how hard they worked to improve their basketball shooting, complete the five-hundred-piece puzzle, or learn how to ride a bike. Children will feel less frustrated with their efforts if we as parents make it clear that getting to the goal usually takes time and numerous attempts. It's also appropriate to say that it's okay when a child decides to walk away from a challenging task. We all need breaks in frustrating endeavors. Focusing on the process of how a child learns also sends the message that they are not valued by the outcome or results of a test or challenge, but rather for simply participating in the process and having their own ideas.

When we as parents inadvertently criticize or judge a child's mistake, struggle, or failure (often with the aim to help them), or even comment on how they are approaching something—"That block's too heavy to make a tower; it won't work"; "Why are you trying to ride your bike that way again?"—we send the message that we think there's something wrong with the child or that they are not capable.

The child hears, "Your ideas, your thinking, is not good. You cannot do it."

The psychologist Wendy Mogel calls it "good suffering" when we let our children sit in uncomfortable feelings or situations. She says, "It's good for [children] to be bored, lonely, disappointed, frustrated, and unhappy." Why? Because they will eventually have to deal with these feelings on their own. Mogel continues, "When we intervene to prevent pain in tough situations, we create a reflex: whenever the child feels any sadness or confusion, frustration or disappointment, [they believe] they cannot survive the feeling." Once again, this calls upon us, the parents, to look into ourselves and ask how we feel about our children experiencing such challenges and emotions.

Habits of the House

Being part of a family also means sharing responsibilities, looking out for each other, and pitching in collectively. The topic of chores comes up frequently with parents wanting to foster a sense of responsibility in their children and get help in the daily needs of the house. Taking part in the tasks of a household matters. I caution parents away from labeling these tasks "chores" and refer to them as "habits of the house," or a related term that fits for your family. Whether you are a family of two or five or more, collectively pitching in and sharing responsibilities unites the family unit and builds important social skills, such as respect and reciprocity. (You'll read more about such social skills in chapter six.) Establishing habits of the house sends the message that "we are all in this together" and teaches children how to participate in activities that benefit a group.

How you set up the structure of your own habits of the house is up to you, but here are some suggestions.

First, identify what needs to get done—for example, setting the table, clearing the plates to the sink, doing dishes (loading the dishwasher if the children are old enough), taking out the trash, getting the mail, emptying the dishwasher, folding or putting away their laundry, feeding or walking the pet, watering plants.

You decide what the shared tasks of your family are. As a child, I was the "vaccuumer" anytime we had to choose our task, which I enjoyed doing for some reason. After deciding on the tasks to be done, come up with a schedule or set of expectations of who does what and when. Different families will distribute the household habits in different ways. You may want to let people choose their tasks or set up a chart or schedule. However you do it, view these habits of the house as responsibilities that everyone takes a part in. There's an implicit flexibility to this approach as well as an opportunity to be cooperative and collaborative—skills all children need in the outside world, from school to work to friendships to home.

It's my experience that children enjoy participating and assuming responsibility, especially when they feel like they are participating in the adult world. Younger children can have small brooms or a small cloth to clean with, and be "just like Mommy or Daddy" or "one of the big kids." It feels empowering to act like the adults do. When my boys were school age, we decided it was time for everyone to do more around the house. Up until that point, they cleared their plates and put their clothes in the hamper; they made their beds in the morning (which varied from a neatly made bed for one to a child who barely pulled up his covers; I left it up to them and made sure to withhold comment or criticism). We had a busy household as many of you do. So I made a chart that I hung up on the wall with three tasks to be completed daily (set table, serve and clear, empty dishwasher) and different children's names on tasks each day, a rotation of sorts. I tried to build in clear expectations with flexibility and clarity—all to no avail. They fought over days, tasks, and who would do what.

Then the two older boys finally said, "Mom, the chart you made up makes no sense! Let us do it ourselves!" and they did. They came up with a system the three of them agreed upon, and I was out of it completely. Every day, the table was set, the dishes were cleared, and the dishwasher was filled and emptied. Habits of the house. What I had overlooked, and they spoke up and showed me, was that they wanted a say in how they would participate and share responsibilities amongst them. By being given this agency, they took on their roles with more responsibility, even if they did not love doing the tasks. Once they started doing it, they never stopped. Habits are just like routines—once we do them every day, we tend to do them every day: put shoes in the shoe bin, coats on the hook, clothes in a hamper, dirty plates in the sink, and so on. Start by identifying the tasks and involving your children in a variety of them. If you have an older child or teen and you are thinking you missed your window to instill these habits, it is not too late. College graduates returning home? What a perfect opportunity!

Habits of the home offer your children an experience of taking responsibility, caring for self and family, and independence. All of these skills are transferable to the outside world as your child grows up. While they may complain or try to negotiate their way out, they will still oblige if the expectations are clear. Believe it or not, doing the tasks can turn to laughter and fun, too.

You can begin with and personalize some of these habits of the home by establishing a set of expectations around self-care, including any of the following (you choose):

- Making their beds
- Putting clothes in the hamper (not on the floor)
- Brushing teeth in the morning and evening
- Hanging up towels in bathroom
- Putting away toys (at least some) or school materials
- Folding or putting away clean laundry

- Keeping their rooms tidy enough
- Doing (or helping to do) laundry
- Clearing the yard, raking, or shoveling snow

I will admit that sometimes it's hard to resist the urge to do household tasks yourself because it will take less time, you want to avoid hearing the complaints, or you simply don't like the way your eight-year-old folds his laundry. Just keep in mind that when you allow your child to participate in tasks around the home, you are giving them an opportunity to be responsible and feel part of your mini-community. Try to let the way they do something go without a negative comment, and I assure you, they will rise to the occasion one of these days. Responsibility and resilience go hand in hand. The more opportunities they have to take on responsibility, the more it will grow. Plus, this is another step toward independence.

How Shame Can Interfere

As parents we don't always support our children's agency or strivings for independence. There are a number of ways that we can inadvertently impede a child's growing independence: we can try to be their friend and forget that we are their parent and they need us to set boundaries; we can give them mixed signals about how independent we think they can be; we can micromanage or be too controlling; we can be clingy and need for them to make us happy or put them in a position of caring for our feelings; we can want them to stay little and forget they need to grow up. But perhaps the most pernicious way we can interfere with our child's growing sense of self and agency is when we shame them, even if we do not mean to. Shame works against a child's naturally emerging self. It works against a child's ability to grow a core sense of who he or she is or the feeling that they have agency and can impact their environment; shame instead instills a corrosive sense of self-doubt. You may be wondering why any parent would shame a child, someone they love.

Most of the time parents don't realize they're doing it; no parent aims to hinder their child's growth. They don't understand that the way they speak to their children, embarrass their children, or attempt to control their children's behavior or criticize it can cause feelings of shame. And being filled with shame can be hard to overcome for children. By trying too hard to direct their children's behavior as an opportunity to teach them about the world, or "for their own good," they undermine their child's tender yet vulnerable growing sense of self.

Think for a moment: Have you ever commented upon or criticized your child's choice of clothing with a less-than-positive attitude about their choices? Spoken about them in front of other parents as if they were not there? Maybe even chuckling as you told a funny story?

We all have likely done this at one time or another, but becoming aware of how this kind of intrusion can happen will go a long way in heeding your own behavior:

- Have you ever lovingly, quietly spoken to your spouse or a good friend in front of your child about his falling out of his big-boy bed or about your eight-year-old still sneaking into your bed at night?
- Have you ever casually hinted to his teacher or another parent that your three-year-old is *still* not potty trained, right in front of him?
- Have you ever reported to a friend that cute statement your child made by mixing up words, while she was within earshot? Whispered about your child's occasional stutter when he was close by and that you thought he would have outgrown it by fourth grade?

- Have you ever looked on in exasperation when you realized you had to change your nine-year-old's wet bed, yet again, as you turned back to go to their bedroom?
- Have you ever said to your child, "You're a big kid now; you don't do this anymore"?
- Have you ever used sarcasm or teased your teen for so-called childish behavior? Or commented, "Really? You are too old for that. You can't just go by yourself?" when your sixteen-year-old asked you to go with them to the dentist?

Often, this kind of inadvertent shaming stems from our own unacknowledged anger, shame, self-doubt, or frustration of feeling less than about ourselves. We bring this baggage into being a parent from our own history and upbringing. The risk here is that when we say something that directly or indirectly shames or embarrasses our children, we make them feel bad, less than, and ashamed for who they are, imperiling their sense of self. Doubts and holes in their sense of agency set in. Instead of addressing the reason a child may be resistant to move from a crib to a bed, we insist they should be big (denying that they also feel little). Rather than recognizing that there could be a reason the child is wildly screaming and laughing, we say, "You're so silly." Instead of realizing that our teen is nervous about a possible cavity and always resists going to the dentist, we say, "Act your age." Our words are powerful. (See chapter seven for further discussion of how to avoid shaming and learn to accept our children for who they are.)

Shame also keeps children from trying new things or asking for help when they need it. Again, most parents do not mean to interfere with their child's march to independence, but it's incumbent upon you to become aware of your use of language and other ways you may inadvertently communicate judgment or criticism or get overinvolved. I like to remind parents that they need to trust their children to grow and develop; it can take time, and the same is true for our teens—what child doesn't want to get out of diapers or Pull-Ups and know how much that will please Mommy or Daddy; what eighteen-year-old is not eager to show a parent they are excited for college or their next step after high school but also has to know that being worried about leaving home is okay? They all grow up eventually, too.

The You Factor

Be aware of your own feelings about your child becoming more independent, especially as they continue to need you, but in changing ways. Parents have their own inner push-and-pull experience: We want our children to grow up and be independent, but this move away from us can feel like a loss. We can experience sadness as our children grow up. We want them to grow close to their friends, but we may feel uncomfortable as if we are being replaced. We may fear the lessening of the intimacy that comes with spending so much time with our children when they are younger as they choose to spend time with friends or participating in their own activities. Indeed, there's a low rumble for many parents when they begin to realize that this goal of raising independent children means they may not need or want us in the same ways they once did.

So how do we manage this gradual release of responsibility without our own feelings getting in the way? How do we back off and stay present for them at the same time? We think of that string of connection, accepting that our parent-child relationship is forever a dynamic of moving toward and moving away.

This dynamic can get complicated. At times, parents' needs clash with those of their children, and often reveal ambivalence on the part of the parents, highlighting the importance of being open to our own feelings and maintaining open communication, as demonstrated in the following example.

Meredith's college-age daughter Naya called to say she was coming home for the weekend for an impromptu visit. This mother was delighted and welcomed the visit, although she already had social plans of her own. As a single mother, Meredith was embracing some of the freedom she had now that Naya was out of the house, and at the same time, she missed having her daughter around and was feeling uncomfortable about how to adjust. When Naya announced her plans, Meredith felt awkward telling Naya that she had plans for most of the weekend. Her assumption was that Naya had plans of her own.

As the busy weekend wound down, her nineteen-year-old became increasingly short-fused, made angry quips to her mother, and was clearly upset. Eventually, Naya complained about not being able to see or spend much time with her and Meredith quickly got defensive: "Well, I didn't know you were coming home, and I had already made my plans!" Inside, this mother was fuming, thinking to herself, *Don't I have a right to have my own plans?! After all, you are away at college now and I raised you practically on my own.* Meredith felt a mixture of irritation and sadness.

Naya replied, "Why didn't you just tell me you were busy before I even came home? I could have changed plans."

Meredith suddenly realized that she, too, had made assumptions, and said, "I am always happy to have you here. I miss you, and I guess I was afraid that you wouldn't come home if I said I had other plans."

"Well, at least give me the opportunity to make my own decision!"

Meredith pulled back.

"You're right. I did not think this through. I was mostly thinking about me and that I wanted you to come home. I'm sorry. Next time I will be more up front about what I am doing."

In this example, there were two sets of needs, some of them

communicated and some of them not. Naya wanted to come home and have time with her mom but had not communicated that need. Maybe it was hard for her to say that she needed mom time at a point in her life when she thought she should be more adult since she was at college. In truth, her weekend visits home from college typically involved time with her friends. Her mother also had conflicting needs. On the one hand, Meredith was excited to see her daughter, but she also resented Naya's assumption that she drop everything. But probably even more important was Meredith's realization that she was having trouble adjusting to Naya no longer living at home. Every step toward independence is a transition—for the child and for the parent.

These conflicting priorities—to be together and to do their own thing—were not communicated by either of them, which led to hurt feelings.

The point here is that parents also have to be aware of their own struggle as their children grow and gain independence. And the groundwork laid in their relationship over the first nineteen years of Naya's life gave them the ability to come back together (the repair that is described in chapter three) following the miscommunications and hurt feelings.

Thank goodness that separation is a mutual process that both parents and children navigate together and in parallel; I like to remind parents of a few things:

- Celebrate the moments of independence along with the moments of togetherness.
- Tune in to moments of closeness and attachment.
- Use narrative to create bridges: "When you were little . . ."; "Remember when . . ."
- Be aware of your own mixed feelings; there can be both pride in their growing up and sadness over their not being little any

longer. Noting the sadness allows you to embrace their next phase.

Helping children gain the freedom that is part of being independent is a long-term goal of parenting. Trust, missteps, support, and parental self-awareness of why it may be hard to let go are all a part of the process of children becoming independent.

REFLECTIVE QUESTIONS

As you contemplate your own experience in relation to your child's separation from you and developing agency, consider these questions:

- Were you raised in a primarily authoritarian (strict), permissive (loose), uninvolved/neglectful, or authoritative (balance of freedom and limits) household?
- Were you punished when you broke the rules or shamed for not following them?
- What was it like if you did something wrong? Were you encouraged to learn from your mistakes and try again? Were you ridiculed or punished? What was that like for you?
- What kind of chores and responsibilities did you have in your home growing up? Recall what parts you liked or did not.
- Were you ever shamed or judged for not doing well in school or not meeting your parents' expectations? Think of an experience and what that felt like to you.
- Did your parents ever let you down or disappoint you in some way? What did that feel like for you?
- Can you recall a time when you were encouraged to try something new? How did this experience make you feel?
- How do you feel about your child growing up, becoming independent, and needing you at more of a distance? Note the positive as well as the negative feelings that you have.

CHAPTER 6

The Power of Connection

Pillar Four: Connecting with Others

Up until this point, we have discussed the importance of connection in a variety of ways—from attachment and separation, to attuning to a child's needs, to the power of listening, holding, comforting, and soothing that we do. The very nature of your relationship with your child is based on an emotional connection, namely love. Yet understanding the depth and nuance of how and why this connection matters is crucial to helping children develop another dimension of their resilience: their ability to connect with others and navigate the social world. After all, no one is meant to live in isolation, and the more confident our children are in social circumstances and the more comfortable they are relating to others in authentic ways, the more likely they will ask for help and turn to support when needed. Being comfortable asking for help is an important factor in their overall resilience.

We all want our children to get along well with other people, form trusting friendships, feel well-liked and socially accepted, and work through problems with siblings and peers when conflicts arise. Social relationships are the ways in which children continue to develop self-esteem, empathy, and the ability to express a difference of opinion, resolve conflicts, and manage repairs of their own.

Helping Others and Asking for Help

When parents come to me nervous or upset about how to help their children navigate the often-complicated social dimension of their lives, especially with peers, their anxiety is often rooted in not fully understanding why this aspect of their children's lives is so important. They grasp that kids need friends and have to get along with others, but why it matters so much is often unclear. In other words, if their child is doing fine otherwise, doing well in school, why does it matter if they don't have a good friend or if they are being left out?

At the most basic level, the social world is about learning. Young children can play by themselves and need ample time to; however, when they do so with other children, there's an added richness and complexity that deepens the learning. The social demands push them to adjust and learn with more attention and nuance. Playing, cooperating, collaborating, compromising, working out conflicts, sharing, taking turns, communicating, and taking another's point of view are inherently social skills that enhance understanding and optimize brain development and functioning, including academic learning and focus. All of these skills enable children to learn about themselves and others in the context of the world around them. Not knowing how to interact with classmates and peers not only excludes them from forming friendships but also prevents them from benefiting from an important learning domain.

This awareness of others as separate people and cuing into how the social world operates is referred to as social cognition. As children mature, they grow in their awareness of their own feelings, thoughts, desires, and motives in the context of other people. Social interactions and experience with peers enable children to gradually come to understand that others have feelings and ideas that can be different from their own. They learn—sometimes through trial and error—how best to respond in certain situations, like when it's okay to speak up or how to compromise without giving up their ideas entirely. Children all benefit from our guidance in understanding when to listen, how to make new friends and choose a reliable friend group, and how to form healthy boundaries.

Interacting with peers and participating in social situations also helps children develop what we call prosocial behaviors—the ability to cue into and care about others leads children to help and care for others. When a child falls down on the playground and another child goes over to help them up, they are demonstrating prosocial behavior. Recognizing another person is sad and asking what they can do to help is another example, or when a teen offers to share their English class notes with a classmate who has been out sick. Volunteering to sweep the kitchen floor after dinner or calling an elderly grandmother are also examples of prosocial skills.

As parents, we can provide messages to our children that both helping others and asking for help for ourselves are valued. You do this in your relationship every day as you provide care, comfort, and support to your child without judging them for what they need. Modeling asking for help is important, too. You can do so by showing your child that you ask for help when needed. It's enormously important that children learn that asking for help is a good thing; indeed, education research has long established that those students who are "help-seeking" are more successful. It's up to us to message that idea and show by our own actions that asking for help is positive, not something to ever be ashamed of. That way our children are able to both grow independently and know when and how to turn to others for assistance.

Giving and receiving help are reciprocal processes. When parents model how to take turns, act generously, and share, children learn how to take turns, be generous, and share. When we model kindness toward others, including our children, we are instilling not only our values but also an opportunity for our children to incorporate this way of being in the world. Conversely, demanding that children share before they are developmentally ready to do so can backfire. Most children are not truly ready to share until they have a strong sense of their own autonomy, around age three or four. But that doesn't mean parents should stop modeling these prosocial behaviors; eventually, children will learn and do them on their own.

Scientists distinguish these kinds of helping behaviors from those that children and adults engage in that are primarily driven by our own needs; prosocial behaviors benefit others, along with ourselves. At a neurobiological level, we are hardwired for such behaviors as individuals rely on the larger group for survival and the group is made up of individuals. The research of UCLA social neuroscientist Matthew Lieberman and others demonstrates how altruistic behaviors are related to a vast network of neural pathways that ultimately reward us—with good feelings, release of oxytocin and dopamine, and optimistic, prosocial feelings. Interestingly, oxytocin and dopamine, the so-called feel-good hormones, are the same two hormones that are released when mothers nurse and care for an infant. Biologists refer to this pair of hormones as attachment hormones—they are the brain-body's way of reinforcing early attachment between mother and child. In other words, helping others feels good and has both an individual and a social purpose.

While we have known for a long time that child development is by and large a social process that begins with the earliest attachment to a primary caregiver, recently neuroscientists have further defined the significance of this social dimension and why it is so key to lifelong development and its relationship to resilience. Specifically, cognitive social neuroscientists have used fMRI methodology to explicate the mental and emotional mechanisms that are set into place through our earliest relationship experiences (e.g., the parent-child relationship) and lay down the wiring that enables and frames how we move in the social world. This exciting work uncovered how the neurobiology of the attachment system is not only foundational to how we interpret and respond to others but also has lifelong implications. For instance, social neuroscientist Lieberman points out, "the same attachment system that causes us to cry as infants when we are separated from our caregiver also causes us to respond to our own baby's cries once we are grown [and become parents ourselves]." The neurobiology of attachment is so strong that it carries over intergenerationally. Lieberman also theorizes that the power of this inborn social mechanism is what in large part made it possible for the evolutionary growth in the size of the human brain. The new connections and brain pathways developed based on the high need of humans to be social expanded the brain—a powerful example of form following function. What does this mean for understanding your child and their developing resilience?

The Roots of Empathy and Compassion

As children learn these prosocial behaviors, they are also understanding that other people have thoughts and feelings different from their own; this is premised on their first establishing and solidifying their sense of self as separate from their parent, as discussed in earlier chapters. I think of the child as moving further out from the parent-child relationship, and, with that loving bond and security residing within them, then opening their eyes wider to who else is in their world. It is at this point—and continuing throughout their lives—that they see other people as individuals, begin to understand who they are, and desire to be with them and to interact.

As you can probably imagine, there will be times when children are more self-focused and other times they are more capable of focusing on the needs of another. Just because your four-year-old was able to work out a solution with his brother, who wanted to build a Lego city when he wanted them to watch TV together, does not mean that a compromise will happen over who gets to pick the afternoon activity on another day. It's also true that balance is needed. Helping without being able to ask for help can lead to being too giving at your own expense and create a depleting habit of putting others before yourself. Giving too much of oneself may, in turn, create other needs, such as a constant need for recognition. We aim for both—the ability to give and to have one's own needs met.

As this understanding of others as separate people grows, children move closer to a crucial ability we refer to as theory of mind, which refers to the capacity to mentalize or imagine what others think or feel. This ability, which children are thought to develop more fully around the age of four, includes being able to imagine another person's mental activity and see it as different from their own. Theory of mind enables children to infer the mental or emotional state of another person based on that person's actions, their facial expressions, or their nonverbal cues. This ability not only helps children learn how to empathize and feel genuine compassion for others, but it also helps them define themselves with more clarity. Children require such contrast with others to understand how they themselves may be similar to or different from people in their lives:

> "Sean and I both like to play Xbox."
>
> "Maura and I both love to get our nails colored blue with green specks."
>
> "Sheree and I like to jump on the trampoline, but Karolina doesn't."
>
> "My sister loves sugary cereal for breakfast, but I don't. I eat toast."

Children are trying to determine who they are in the context of others, which promotes understanding of others as well as a growing self-awareness. Being able to understand oneself in the context of other people allows children to know their strengths and see themselves as separate but perhaps different from others. This self-awareness ultimately supports their being resilient in the face of feeling different from but not less than others. As you will see in the next chapter, self-awareness is what allows a child to grow a clear sense of identity and self-acceptance—all of which are foundational to being resilient in the face of obstacles, crises, or uncertainties.

How to Model Social Skills

As a parent you may assume that learning social skills is intuitive and that your children's growing independence means that they are equipped with the knowledge of how to listen, act appropriately, share, and cooperate with others, regardless of the social situation. You may think that in time they will grow these skills, yet children can at times benefit from explicit scaffolding and guidance from adults to develop, practice, and deepen these social skills. Preteens, adolescents, and young adults also benefit from our help as they manage intense emotions and complex or novel social situations throughout their lives, including romantic relationships, job interviews and workplace behavior, and other, more formal social situations.

Many colleges and universities, including where I have spent my academic career, provide this kind of explicit scaffolding for students as they step further into the adult world. We help students prepare for job interviews with mock interviews to give them a sense of what to expect and how to respond to a range of potential questions and interactions, right down to guidance on what to wear. We have workshops on how to act in workplace settings and interact on teams, and how to handle conflict with a supervisor or coworker.

Similarly, in a yearlong intensive child development course I lead each year, I teach students how to work in small groups. While this is part of their coursework, from conducting research projects to addressing topics in child development, I frame these group interactions as preparation for life. More broadly, it is an opportunity to learn valuable skills in negotiating, building consensus, listening to others, and being heard. We take a similar approach at the child development center I oversee. When student assistants begin their work with the children, teachers provide clear guidelines: when to arrive, why being on time matters to the flow of the day, how to work with their teammates and support one another, how to ask for help, how to interface with parents, and what is expected of them for setup and cleanup. These concrete details are guidelines on expected behavior that young adults still need to get their footing in new situations and to free them up to learn about how children develop.

Step back for a moment and you may realize that we all need such guidance sometimes: What is expected of me? How do I handle this new situation? Do people take lunch breaks at this new job and at what time? We sometimes forget that even our older child needs continued guidance and teaching of social skills and expectations, especially as they first enter into more adult situations. So when you think about how you do this for your own children, we start again with your relationship. Your interactions, kindness, limits, and responsiveness are all teaching them how to treat others and how they should expect to be treated themselves. Layered upon that are the myriad of more intentional ways that you help enhance social skills in your daily interactions.

In the following list I highlight a variety of ways that you can build on what you already do with your child to further enhance their socialization abilities. While some of the suggestions will likely sound obvious to you, I always like to remind parents, too, that children benefit from explicit instruction and lots of repetition and practice as well. Do this proactively, and it can become part of routines and habits:

- Role-play. Have fun as you teach social skills. Learning these vital skills does not have to be onerous. One suggestion is to engage children in role-playing scenarios to practice different or novel social scenarios and interactions. Children four and up tend to enjoy this. Develop a range of different strategies and outcomes to help them feel competent in handling a variety of situations and entering new ones. Role-playing can boost their confidence, especially for your hesitant, anxious, or slower-to-warm-up child. Skills you can focus on include taking turns, sharing, entering into play with other children (a key skill for success in the peer domain), problem-solving and resolving conflicts ("You are with three friends who all have different ideas about how to build the structure you are planning together; let's play this out"), or expressing emotions appropriately ("Let's pretend we ran out of your favorite cookies and now you are mad; what are three ways you could show that?" And then go over the scenarios, which ones would convey which emotions and how to communicate better—and why). It is also good to propose situations where a friend wants something different from or in direct opposition to what your child wants. Together you can derive possible solutions on what could be done, without focusing on one right way but helping your child to elicit several possible outcomes. Ask, "How do you think that would work? How would your friend (or sibling) feel?" The aim is to give them experience with resolving situations where they can see another perspective that is different from their own. Play them out and have fun with it, too.

• Demonstrate good social skills yourself. Again, you are your child's best role model. When you are polite and show respect to a salesclerk at the local grocery store or the server in a restaurant, they learn that this is a respectful way to interact with and treat people. When you work out a disagreement with a partner over what to eat for dinner, they observe how to resolve conflicts. When you cook a meal for a neighbor who recently came home from the hospital, they learn to show care at times of need. All of these are behaviors of respect and caring that they learn from observing you.

• Make up stories, tell real stories, or use picture books that focus on social situations and emotions. These stories can help children understand tricky situations; what behaviors they can (and can't) use, and why; perspective taking; and how to navigate social interactions effectively. Ask how a character feels or what they might do differently in response to a situation in a book or video. You can tie these examples to their own lives. For example, "This sounds like when your friend Keegan didn't want to meet you after school; do you remember what that felt like?" Tween and teen literature often deals with friendship conflicts and provides a way to connect to your older child's social world as well; chat with them about what they are reading or viewing and what they think. Even when the book, video, or story resolves the situation, you can ask about the resolution as well as the other possible ways the characters could have responded. You might even delve into scenarios that are not appropriate, and why considering all possibilities is part of full understanding. When you consider these joint discussions, you may be surprised to hear all that your teen is thinking about. It should not be set up as a way to scold, criticize, or judge them but to learn more about their social world and to provide support and guidance. Keep one tip in mind: the more you listen without feeling the need to correct them, the more they will be willing to talk.

• Play games that require teamwork and cooperation. Games teach important skills like taking turns, jointly establishing and following rules, and working together toward a common goal. There are fun, cooperative games that have a common team goal (finding a hidden/lost treasure, for example) and also places like escape rooms where the whole family has to cooperate to find their way out. In games, even when they are noncompetitive, players still need to agree on decisions, strategies, or routes to take as a team, which builds negotiating, flexibility, and cooperation skills as well, all in the context of having fun. You may want to try doing silly activities together like squiggle drawing: One family member draws a squiggle on the paper. Another adds their own squiggle to it (try different colors), and then another, and a fun and creative image emerges, a family collaboration. All ages can do this. You can decide to name the emerged image or build on it by making up a story about it once it is complete. The point is to have fun and be aware that there are skills being built secondarily.

• Intentionally and explicitly teach children effective communication skills, in addition to modeling them. For example, verbally note your role in active listening ("I am listening to you; can you tell me more?"). To help them improve their listening and communication skills, I encourage you to think about when you are using your phone or other device, which can distract you from being present with your child or divide your attention. Technology is intertwined deeply in our lives, and we need to be aware of when it may be interfering with our ability to stay attuned to our children. Supporting your child when they may need help in hearing another person's viewpoint also helps build their communication skills: "Your friend is asking you to hear what she is saying; see if you can pause for a moment and listen to her. It sounds like she does not want to do that game." Help children express themselves assertively but respectfully: "You can tell him that you don't like that." "You can tell her to stop." "So your friend did that and you were upset. What do you want to say to them to help them know how much it upset you?"

- Teach children problem-solving skills, emphasizing the importance of finding win-win solutions and how and when to compromise. Often, children think they will somehow lose if they agree with another person's side in the midst of a disagreement. Help them see what compromise is and that both they and their friend or sibling can arrive at a mutual decision, even when that means giving up something. Guide them through the process of identifying the problem, brainstorming a range of possible solutions, and evaluating the consequences of their potential actions. Try not to be taken aback when they come up with what might seem like an unreasonable solution ("I am just going to tell his other friend never to play with him anymore!") and ask them how they think the other person might respond, helping them understand the potential impact of their words and actions on others.

- Plan social outings and playdates for younger children and encourage your older child or teen to reach out to their friends; children benefit from interacting with peers outside of structured, rules-based settings where adults are in charge. Letting them decide on what to do, how to do it, and how they want to interact or play when they are together helps them with decision-making, problem-solving, and organization skills. Suggest outdoor locations for such get-togethers, including parks, backyards, and local hiking trails, where no one "owns" the space. Encourage them to initiate conversations, practice getting along, share materials together, and engage in cooperative play. Cooking is an activity that children can work on together; it takes collaboration with the bonus that they can eat their outcome. Younger children can cook with supervision; teens can plan and carry out cooking together. This was a favorite activity of my then–high schooler and a group of friends during the pandemic. They loved the planning involved in deciding on a meal, making a list of ingredients, going to the store to purchase what they needed, and then preparing, serving, and enjoying the meal. They continue to meet up when they are home from college for these collective meals and still love this great way to socialize.

Patience is key here, though it can be hard to remember at times—these skills take time, practice, and plenty of missteps and are not all learned at once. Progress at one point can be followed by a step backward at another time. During times of upset, stress, or uncertainty, even the best of us can forget to mind our manners or be at our best to notice what others want or need.

Children with Difficulty Reading Social Cues

Parents of children with autism spectrum disorder often ask me for advice on how to help their children learn to read social situations and respond appropriately. I believe strongly that with consistent, explicit instruction, many children on the ASD spectrum can learn to become more socially and emotionally competent, especially when they are offered explicit instruction and support around social situations.

Here are some suggestions:

- Engage children in structured play activities that encourage social interaction. This could include cooperative board games, building projects, or group activities with clearly defined roles and rules. Structured play provides a safe and supportive environment for children to practice social skills and emotional understanding. Openly talk about what a friend or family member is asking of them so they can practice reading others' social and emotional facial cues.

- Create a sensory-friendly environment that minimizes sensory distractions and provides necessary supports, such as noise-canceling headphones or a quiet space for breaks if needed. Helping them handle their emotions in socially appropriate ways, through taking frequent breaks if necessary, aids children with emotion regulation, which in turn will help them become better able to participate in groups.

- Try a social-emotional skills learning program that teaches specific skills step by step. These programs focus on skills like initiating conversations, maintaining eye contact, taking turns, and showing and understanding nonverbal and emotional cues.

- Practice social interactions using scripts or phrases they can use in specific situations. Engage in role-playing activities to simulate real-life scenarios, allowing them to practice appropriate responses, turn-taking, and problem-solving. For younger children these groups are play based, and I have seen children make great strides that they take back into their daily interactions. Groups for older children and teens also exist.

- I interface with a program in New York City called the Meeting House, founded and run by Paula Resnick and staffed by a warm and skilled team of professionals. They run after-school programs for all ages, using a social and emotional learning model that builds community and focuses on children learning about themselves and how to get along with peers through play and collaborative projects. Look for similar places in your area or look up their online resources. They have a wonderful blog that focuses on issues including empathy, care, community, and conflict resolution, all aimed at understanding how to support children. Their post about 50 Social Essential Social Skills (for all ages) is excellent and defines the many skills that go into socializing and managing emotions.

- Encourage interactions with neurotypical peers who can serve as positive role models. Pairing a child with ASD with a peer buddy can provide guidance, support, and mutual friendship while engendering greater acceptance for the peer.

- Introduce the concepts of Social Thinking (www .socialthinking.com), a research-informed curriculum developed by Michelle Garcia Winner that offers resources, practical strategies, and visual tools for neurodivergent and neurotypical children of all ages. This program and its offerings are used widely by teachers, speech-language pathologists, counselors, therapists, and parents to help neurodiverse and children on the autism spectrum learn to recognize social cues and participate in social experiences.

Every child with ASD is a unique person, and their social skills needs will vary. It's important to find support to tailor interventions and strategies to meet the specific needs and strengths of your individual child. It's also helpful to involve or collaborate with professionals such as occupational therapists, speech-language pathologists, or behavior therapists who specialize in working with children with ASD. They can provide valuable guidance, individualized interventions, and support for social and emotional skill development.

Belonging and Fitting In

What is being socially adept all about? It's about learning how to get along well with others, listening and responding thoughtfully, and otherwise respecting the viewpoints of others, whether people who share similarities or people who do not. It is also about knowing your own voice and how to articulate what you need to others. As discussed, an important skill that children learn is what is referred to as "perspective taking"—the ability to understand and accept that another person can have a differing point of view from yourself. This is the root of empathy and compassion. These skills are also what enable young people to grow confidence in forming and maintaining relationships with peers, siblings, and you. Taking another's perspective and articulating your needs are part of building resilience.

When parents are involved in their communities and provide opportunities for children to participate, they learn not only how to connect and respect others but also how the sense of belonging makes them feel part of something larger than themselves. There is also reward in giving to others and doing for others. They learn about themselves and other people, breaking down boundaries caused by perceived differences (stereotypes), and forging relationships outside of the family unit. They learn about themselves and how they relate to people of different backgrounds, finding out what they have in common. If there are new people moving into your neighborhood, going over to welcome them with a card your children made and cookies you baked or got from the local bakery is a good way to model reaching out and connecting.

Being part of a community not only helps children get along with other people but also motivates them to balk at prejudice, help others who have fewer resources or who are in need, and form an inclusive attitude toward people generally. These are all values that become part of their community and society and can benefit everyone who lives in them, including your child.

Every person has a basic human need to belong. This instinctive drive to be in affinity with others is tied to our being inherently social beings, able to survive better when we are affiliated with and part of a group. Parents often worry about how well their child fits in with their peers at school or in the neighborhood, and they worry about whether they have any friends, the right friends, or even enough friends. I get it. Wanting our children to have good friendships, including a trusted and loyal confidant, is an aspect of being social that nearly every parent values. However, parents can fall into a trap of overreacting or catastrophizing social situations, especially if it reminds them of a time when they felt they didn't belong or were outright rejected.

I find the peer realm brings up more recollections from parents' pasts than almost anything else. So although our children will benefit from our support as they navigate the playground, school, teen dating, and other complex social situations, we also need to be mindful of maintaining healthy boundaries that encourage our children to figure out how to navigate the intricacies of the social world on their own. It is what gives them the opportunity and space to learn how to understand the nuances of social situations and feel more confident. Children need to test and sort through the messy feelings of vulnerability and fear of rejection at the same time that they want to be liked or fit in with their friends.

Here's an example of just how complex social situations can be for children. Ricky, age seven, came home from school visibly upset, kicking his shoes off angrily. He immediately launched into a fury, yelling, "There's a new kid in my class!"

His mother, Clare, asked a few basic questions—who the child was, their name, whether they just moved there.

Ricky stormed off with a short and clear, "I don't know, and I don't care!"

Clare was surprised about his strong reaction, which seemed out of character for him. Then she decided to give him a chance to settle down.

Soon he came out of his room and cozied himself next to his mother on the couch. He recounted how this new classmate was playing with his best friend, Kenji, at recess and Ricky expressed his worry that the new child would take his friend away from him.

This change in the makeup of the class and peers was rattling to him. Newness readily breeds uncertainty, and in the social domain, that can take on an even deeper concern for a child regarding whether they will be liked and if and how they will fit in. Will a new child take away their other friends, as in this scenario?

Clare wondered aloud about whether the next day Ricky could suggest that the three of them play together.

Ricky responded with a quick and firm "No!" He was upset and irritated.

At first Clare was uncomfortable seeing her son so upset and considered calling Kenji's mom and trying to see if she could help with the situation from the back end. She knew this mom and figured they could work it out for the boys. She hesitated and instead took a breath and decided to step back a bit. In thinking about it, Claire realized that she would be far more helpful to Ricky if she didn't butt in, but simply showed him she cared and could empathize with his feelings given the situation.

She simply said, "This is upsetting, I can tell." Then she listened to him vent and gave him time to sit with the dilemma and to be in his emotions.

By dinner that night, Ricky's outlook began to change. He came up with a plan on his own to organize a game the next day so the three classmates could play together. But the slight worry about what would happen remained in the morning when it was time for school. With reassurance from his mother that she thought they'd work out a way to play, he went to school and later reported having a good time at recess.

What this example illustrates is the need for us, as parents, to be aware of ourselves and know when not to interfere or overstep. The mother signaled her support and empathized with her son, while also respecting his need to storm off and vent. When he returned, she listened and empathized. In the end, her sticking close by but not interfering gave him the space to come up with his own plan and feel successful. The positive outcome was something he could hold on to and that would feed into his growing resilience, the feeling that he could get through rough moments, this time involving a good friend.

When a child strives to fit in, they often experience a contrasting desire to stand apart from the crowd and assert their individuality. Some more so than others. You may have a child who likes to be different—such as a three-year-old who came to my program every session in unmatched shoes and pajamas; or the teenager who gets a drastic haircut or dyes their hair bright purple. Managing these gestures can be confusing to all of us at times—and it becomes especially tricky when children enter adolescence and later on in the young adult years.

Here's an example. Wanda was a talented art student at her high school, thinking about going to art school in the future, and had recently won a highly regarded community award for her outstanding mixed-media collages. She prided herself on her artistic talents and she valued the recognition she received from teachers and adults, but she had few close friends. Her sense of style came through in her clothes as well, with bright colors and scarves, and she spent extra time each morning picking out earrings, some of which she made herself. Her parents embraced her style and told her how they admired her creativity. So they were surprised when she came home one afternoon, quieter than usual, and after a long dinner of mostly silence (except snapping at her brother to leave her alone) she revealed that "I just don't fit in. I have no friends." She went to her room and closed the door, saying she wanted to be left alone.

What threw her parents the most was that she had always shown an independent streak, dressing how she wanted with confidence and building her creative style, which appeared to come quite naturally to her. They followed her lead, letting her pick her clothes and taking her to buy unique fabrics to make accompanying headbands and scarves. And yet, as a teenager, Wanda was discovering that being different did not always feel good. True, she liked the attention for her art and creativity at times, but at other times she "just wanted friends" and "to be like other kids," as she told her father later. He was at a bit of a loss as he'd thought allowing her to be herself and supporting her unique ways was enough. What the parents did not pick up on was her longing to fit in and have friends her age who understood her—not just adults who admired her, although that was nice.

This example reflects the tension many young people experience between wanting to be their own person and wanting to fit in. When I spoke to Wanda's parents, I suggested that they encourage Wanda to seek out other ways she might explore her art. After doing some research together, Wanda decided to take part in an after-school program for kids who were dealing with stressful life situations. Wanda's job was to teach pottery to a group of fifth graders, and she loved it. She felt as if she had an adult role with the children, which was a boost for her. Not only did she find it rewarding to interact with the children, she also made new friends at the center. This role and her new friends made her feel accepted and valued for her talents, which countered her sense of not fitting in at school, and gradually she began to once again feel more comfortable at school, too. When she consciously embraced her strengths and interests, Wanda felt more grounded in herself, a hallmark of resilience. Her parents' support and encouragement to seek out options to explore and express her creativity helped her do this, too.

In general, the tension between who a teenager is and what the crowd is doing (the desire to be accepted) can be hard as children move into adolescence and refine and define who they are in the world. It is that feeling of wanting to be invited to a social event even if you don't actually want to attend. Just knowing they could be part of it may be what the person seeks, even as they define themselves as different. Parents can help ease these tensions by listening to their worries and struggles or simply being there as a sounding board, reminding them that you love them no matter what. Once again, this is the parent acting as a container for their still-growing child who is actively building their resilience.

Peer Pressure Is Not the Problem

Adolescence is considered a critical period when social skills take on a new importance for how young people cultivate friendships, how they react to peer pressure, and *how* they manage the conflicts between their pull to fit in and belong and the equally strong push to be independent and autonomous, their own person, to have their own identity. Many parents worry about their children being influenced by the "wrong crowd" and may, as a result, try to interfere and do some "social editing." This will very likely backfire.

Work by Joe Allen, an eminent psychology researcher at the University of Virginia, offers important insight into this complex process of adolescent social and personal development and the role of parents. In his twenty-plus-year longitudinal study following the same 165 teens from ages 13 to 30, Allen identified specific factors that predict success in later adolescence and map onto positive adult relationships and life success over fifteen years later. What is critical about this work is that indicators of success for adolescents, namely genuine close relationships with peers, also map onto adults and how they develop resilience, maintain good health, and prosper in most areas of their lives. Those with more superficial peer relationships in early adolescence did not manage as well, including suffering from depression at higher rates, lacking motivation and confidence, and experiencing poorer health.

Teens are literally wired to play out exactly what they need to learn through their friendships, their peer entanglements, and the erratic ups and downs of relationships. And what they need to learn—the veritable goal of adolescence—is how to balance their need for autonomy with the simultaneous drive to connect in real, thoughtful, sustained ways with their peers. Allen refers to this as the "adolescent dilemma," which was highlighted in a central revelation of his research looking at the so-called cool kids compared to teens who had strong but fewer friendships and fewer of the pseudo-adultlike behaviors of the cool kids. He found that children who were considered "cool" at twelve to fourteen years old may have been considered popular but they also grew up to be less successful, less well adjusted, less healthy, and, yes, less happy than the ones who were not so popular as teens. He found that those young teens who were able to form solid, trusting friendships and did not seek popularity for its own sake fared better.

So why did the teen group that did less well in the long run turn out to be those who were considered "cool" earlier in their lives? The study findings suggest that those adolescents were drawn to quantity of friends, an external indicator of popularity, over quality of genuine friendship connection; their necessary social/emotional roots were more superficial and not as deep as the other teens; and ultimately, their adult-looking "cool" behaviors (drinking, smoking, earlier sex) were more of a mask for a lack of true security and confidence. In other words, while they looked independent and adultlike in behavior, they actually were neither autonomous nor connected in a deep way, which are the factors needed to thrive as teens are traversing the path into early adulthood.

So how can parents help their children resist the urge to go for quantity over quality?

While children striving to become young adults need space and freedom, they still need those guardrails. They also need parent attention and availability. In my experience, the parents who dug in and stayed close emotionally were able to support their adolescents during what can be a turbulent social time. Since you are no longer in the role of organizing and managing playdates, you still want to keep an eye out, being ready to support your teen when they need you, and sometimes that means being there, but holding your tongue, which can be tough.

You may be wondering how you guide without interfering or critiquing. You are in a position to support their autonomy seeking and stay connected, albeit in a background role. At these ages you are not the one choosing their friends, but where you live and who you socialize with in terms of adult friends or other social and community groups has an influence on your teen. They will get to know your friends and hear their ideas and values, and knowing them opens the possibility of mentors. Having mentors outside of their family—teachers, clergy, community members—offers them additional role models. As a teenager, I had a neighbor down the street, a new mother, with whom I spent time in the evenings. I would hear about her paths in life, her career and family choices as she took interest in my ideas and listened to my ups and downs with friends, family, and school as well. Plus, we laughed and had fun. I watched her move from being a public defender to parent and gained confidence by helping her navigate this new adult role. The respect shown by a good mentor reinforces a teen's burgeoning autonomy, builds confidence through the respect shown to them, and can help hone new skills depending on the tasks involved in the mentorship. It is another way that the adolescent can be slowly introduced to what is expected as they become adults. Part-time jobs can take on this role as well.

But parents are not out of the picture; importantly, they remain in the background, to come home to, to be a sounding board and a guide. Teens still want to know their check-in person, their secure base is available when they want them, so stepping back does not mean stepping away entirely. Providing a welcoming and nonjudgmental home for your teenager and their friends is part of this, making it an inviting place for your children to come into if you are open to having friends in your home. If you prefer not to host, invite your high schooler to join in a weekend activity such as hiking or camping; find movies you enjoy together; or spend time together at a sports event or concert. One of my children was a regular companion to visit photo exhibits, another liked to explore a variety of food markets and find hidden nature places in the city. While they were with friends most of the time, the moments we had together still mattered. Respecting your child and connecting to their areas of interest (rather than trying to force your own) shows them you see what they enjoy and respect that. With one of my sons, we found many Magic: The Gathering card shops in cities all over the country, a way we showed how much we respected his passion.

There are two other findings from Allen's large study that can help guide parents, and these may surprise you. The first is that allowing your teen to argue with you can have profoundly positive outcomes when done well. Allen's research found that parents who "allow their teens to negotiate with them when there's a disagreement," using a friendly or nonadversarial, noncombative style, rather than cutting them off with a no-discussion prohibition, had teens who were able to take these skills into interactions with peers. What does this mean? They did not have to give in to peer pressure; they could hold their own ground in saying no when they did not want to do something such as use alcohol or drugs. They had learned effective arguing skills and felt a strength in themselves by having the hidden opportunity to disagree with their parents, typically over grades, curfews, or household chores. By giving room for their teenagers to potentially change their parents' minds about an issue that's important to them—whether that's getting a new cell phone, going to a concert or rave, or staying over at a friend's house with no parents at home—the teens had a stronger base for standing up to negative peer influences.

Allen explains that this two-step approach works because parents set up two key expectations that teens can take into their relationships with peers: first, that it's worth trying to persuade others to do what they want, and second, that this will take actual persuasion. And yet, the limit is there, as the parent will be the decision-maker ultimately, based on the discussion, and that is a boundary for the teenager. Further, not everything is up for discussion, such as basic decency in how family members treat one another. When this is done in a healthy manner, and not over every disagreement, teens feel respected and are able to hone their voice—two keys to their sense of agency, and therefore resilience.

It provides them with an opportunity to figure out what they want or need and how to articulate that. It can help them with perspective taking; understanding your view on the topic is needed to negotiate their side and shows your respect for their opinions. It is the opposite of following the crowd. I suspect that being on a debate team can further support these skills as well.

In contrast, the teen who is never or rarely given the learning opportunity to negotiate with parents—the teen for whom "because I said so, and no is a firm no" is the beginning and the end of the discussion—is used to simply going along with what others say or demand. Alas, while this kind of strict parenting might seem like it would shield teens from peer influence, in reality the opposite occurs. "Yes, sir" and "Yes, ma'am" at home morph into "Well, okay, I have no room for my opinion anyway," conveying defeat or resignation as they've learned at home. So when peers suggest drinking or vandalism or sexual experimentation that a teen might not be comfortable with, they are more likely to defer to the style they know—"Well, okay." Allen refers to them as the "doormat teens." Their voices have been silenced, making it easy to walk over them and gain conformity, even to norms a parent would prefer not to be followed.

Parents do not do this knowingly; I believe every parent is trying to protect their child or teen from harm. Your own fears may get you to be harsher than even you would like, including cutting off discussions. Becoming aware of the patterns identified in this decades-long work—that what is learned in family is taken into peers—is an important step to make parenting changes and be certain you are supporting your teen as they move further into the world on their own. Your relationship still matters.

How Not to Take Things Personally

I was speaking one day with Tonya, the mother of Jasmine, a nine-year-old who frequently brought home stories of interactions with her classmates. Jasmine had always been an observer of her friends, even as a preschooler: "Today Leo did not want to have snack, so he sat and watched instead; Marly did not want to play with Will today—she wanted to be alone." As Jasmine got older, she commented on the more complex interactions her classmates had and could be quite animated in the storytelling of what had happened and who was involved. She emphasized a range of interactions and reactions she had—being liked, being left out or on the sidelines, standing back watching her friends, wanting to play, or not wanting to play. Like others her age, she had a tendency to get fixated on one particular set of friends, a threesome (herself included) where one friend, Lila, often paired with another and excluded the third. The friends Lila picked varied day to day and involved whispers behind the other friends' backs. Jasmine would comment on how her peers behaved and interacted, and how they would sometimes include her and other times not. During the moments Jasmine felt excluded, her mother noticed that her daughter talked about Lila and fixated on the dynamic over and over by repeatedly returning to the scenarios and going through the steps of an interaction as she tried to understand what had happened that day.

"Is this obsessive behavior?" Tonya asked me. "I try to listen and distract her," but she was ready to suggest that Jasmine speak to the school counselor.

Now, in third grade, Jasmine told her mother that Lila had sent a text that "was not nice."

On her own initiative, Jasmine announced that she would talk to the teacher about the situation. She did not want to name the friend, but she planned to ask the teacher if she would talk to the class about texts and address the fact that saying mean things on a text was hurtful, just like saying it in person to someone.

Tonya agreed that the text was not nice (it was about who was and was not this child's friend); she validated her own child's opinion and feelings on it, and then asked if she wanted her to get involved.

"No!" exclaimed Jasmine. "My teacher will help me. And besides, it fits into my manuals."

Tonya was stumped. "What are your manuals?"

Jasmine explained: "Mommy, I have a manual for each friend. One for each; I think I have eleven. For one friend, the manual says that when she won't talk to me, I go back to my work and don't let it bother me. Then she'll talk to me later.

"For my other friend, my cousin, the manual says, she likes to express a lot, and now I am used to that. I wait for her to express everything, and then we can go back to playing together. That's just who she is."

The child continued to explain her understanding of different friends, their styles, and how she herself responded to their actions. Tonya listened to these astute descriptions and then asked her daughter what it would be like if she did not have those manuals (which this mother was hearing about for the first time). Jasmine replied, "Mommy! You know that would not be good! I would think about it too much, like I used to do, and talk about it all the time. It did not feel good for me. Now I have my manual, so I can say, 'Oh, this is how she acts, and this is what I do.' Then I am done, and I can play or go back to doing my schoolwork, but it does not bother me anymore."

When Tonya came to me with this story, she wanted to know if the manuals were normal. "What does it mean that Jasmine created such manuals?"

This was novel for me, too, and I found it to be a brilliant idea, especially for a nine-year-old, and one that inspired me to add it to my repertoire of suggested social strategies. Although the child did not realize it, she was not only protecting herself from being hurt by a friend's moodiness and unpredictable behaviors, she was also learning a valuable skill: not to take the behavior, moods, or the affect of others personally. Further, Jasmine's manuals gave her a way to understand complex and at times confusing social dynamics. Depersonalizing other people's behavior, whether our child's, a friend's, or a partner's, is setting a healthy boundary, and she had come up with a concrete way to do this.

The You Factor

As we've seen, the bond between parent and child develops in a range of different ways—through physical touch and being in proximity, which convey your care and presence; through the tenor and exchange of your emotions; through listening and being available and attentive. These are all types of social interactions as well as emotional. Within the container of your relationship, your child develops the inner sense that they are cared for and worthy of love, an internalized model they can take into relationships with peers and the broader social world. In a secure attachment, children learn that relationships are rewarding and that connection comes from giving of themselves, caring about others, and being cared for in return. They also learn how to manage their emotions and build confidence, and how to get what they need and compromise.

All of these skills are crucial to their ability to move into the complicated world of peers, to get along well with others, resolve conflicts, share, and collaborate. The relationship we have with our child gives them an important model, showing them what relationships look and feel like, what they can expect from others and give to them as well. With this "social knowing" in place, children develop a sense of belonging to something that is larger than themselves—a family, a school, a team, a community—which is inherently critical to our very survival. We hear about the alarming rise of isolation and loneliness, what the US surgeon general termed "an epidemic of loneliness," and the data show that being without reliable relationships and social experiences is tied to increased depression and mental and physical health challenges and even to poorer academic success. We are meant to be with others in social connection.

Our histories and experiences related to social relationships also play a part and may unwittingly affect how we help (or hinder) our children as they build their own social skills. On the one hand, it's important to separate your own experience from what your child encounters. Just because you may have been bullied or made fun of as a child doesn't mean that the same will happen to your child. If you loved being the popular kid in middle or high school, it doesn't follow that your child is similarly extroverted. In order to both stay connected to our children throughout their growing up and provide the guidance and support they need to develop their own social confidence, we need to stay aware of our own experience and avoid projecting it onto our children.

REFLECTIVE QUESTIONS

Becoming aware of our own social experience can help us relate to our children as they navigate the often-tricky world of peers and adults. Consider the following questions:

- How does your own temperament or style affect your interactions with other people, such as family members or close friends? Acquaintances? Coworkers?
- What do you recall about your own peer interactions as a child or teen? Were you ever left out, rejected by other children, or had a hard time fitting in? What was that like for you?
- Did you have a close friend or friends? What do you recall from that relationship?

- How do you ask for help when you need it? Do you see your children modeling this help-seeking? Think about your style with your child when it comes to their social relationships. Are you able to actively listen with your child, or do you prefer to jump in with advice? How does your child respond to you at these times?
- How do you model reciprocity in your own relationships with others? What is the give-and-take you do with friends, relatives, or a partner?
- When your child is having social conflict, how do you respond? For example, do you step in quickly or get involved in your child's disagreements with siblings or friends?
- How do you respond when your child reports being left out or hurt by a friend or classmates? How does it make you feel to hear of these situations?
- How do you respond when your child reports being mean or acting negatively with a friend? How do you feel when you hear of their behavior?
- When your child talks about friends you don't particularly care for, how do you respond? Can you stay aware of your less-than-positive opinions and still listen and support them?
- What do you do when your teenager wants to vent openly about all the bad stuff going on? Are you able to listen and let them vent? Do you quickly try to problem-solve? How does your teen respond to you?

CHAPTER 7

The Gift of Acceptance

Pillar Five: Being Understood

Every person, from child to adult, desires and deserves to be understood and accepted for who they are in all their facets—the good, the bad, and everything in between. It is this acceptance that enables us to like and ultimately love ourselves. By loving and accepting ourselves, we become people who can care for and give to others. When we as parents offer this understanding and acceptance to our child, we give them an enormous gift that will keep giving for the rest of their lives. We show them that loving oneself is about becoming aware of and learning to accept both their positive qualities and their less-than-stellar attributes. We show them that part of accepting who they are is acknowledging their limitations or vulnerabilities. We encourage them to develop a forgiving, loving view of themselves, not so they won't try for betterment but because when they internalize a sense of being seen and loved for who they are, they feel whole. This comprehensive and realistic view of themself positions them to be more ready and able to face challenges because they have a broader and more accurate understanding of what they can and can't do, what it will take to persevere through a challenge, and how to develop the resources (like asking for help when needed) to accomplish their goals.

This final pillar builds on and encompasses the other four pillars of resilience and the ways you've been practicing being your child's anchor and container. You have had the opportunity to help them develop a sense of this wholeness by:

- Instilling an inner safety—you are enabling them to trust you and themselves, knowing at a deep level that they are not alone in the world
- Helping to co-regulate their emotions—you are teaching them how to self-regulate and subsequently handle their own emotions; in turn, they are learning how to stay steady in themselves during times of uncertainty
- Giving them space with guardrails—you are empowering them to separate and become autonomous, able to act with agency and become their own person able to weigh choices and make their own decisions with confidence
- Staying deeply connected—you are equipping them with the know-how to form and be in relationships, communicate directly, and connect with others outside of your family circle in genuine and meaningful ways

The culmination of these pillars comes to fruition when you consciously and knowingly accept your child for who they are, without judgment or shame; by embracing their differences and complexities, you enable your child to embrace themselves with confidence, respect, and the understanding that they matter.

Pillar five distills the ultimate significance of your relationship with your child and why this is so key for developing resilience. Think back to the early chapters on attachment and separation. There is ongoing communication from you to your child throughout this letting-go process, that you see what they need and will address it. Even when you are unsure and struggle to understand them, you can still communicate that you are doing your best to be available for them and not blame, punish, shame, or ridicule their struggles (nor blame yourself). When the messages you communicate are positive and accepting, even and especially when they may be moving through the world very differently from you or how you imagined they might, your child will develop a sense of self that can grow to full acceptance of themselves. They do not develop a harsh inner critic, which can be toxic to their well-being; they don't put themselves down and feel riddled with shame. Instead, they accept their strengths and weaknesses and like who they are because the overall consistent and clear message you've given them is that they are worthy and understood and you love them for who they are.

Ultimately, this deep knowledge of their intrinsic value is one of the most powerful resources of resilience. A child who feels truly seen and appreciated for simply being themselves will rely on this center for the rest of their lives. They will be grounded in themselves, not driven to compare themselves to others in order to measure their self-worth. They will understand how to and will want to care for themselves. They will be loving and compassionate toward their own imperfections and work toward change in themselves—not because they think they are a bad person, but because they want to improve for themselves. In this way, self-acceptance is tied to developing inner motivation.

As parents, we have an enormous opportunity to expedite our children's path to self-acceptance. When we show our children that we love them unconditionally, they internalize the knowledge that they don't have to do anything or prove themselves to us to earn our love. Nurturing self-acceptance in our children begins as they separate and we help them to develop their sense of self, an abstract yet very real experience of one's inner life. A sense of self is related to identity and self-image, though it's not restricted to the way we look or how we feel. A sense of self is that inner knowing of who we are—as Thich Nhat Hanh, the Buddhist philosopher, says, coming into awareness of one's self is like "finding a home in our bodies."

Guiding our children to find this inner home enables them to discover the truly marvelous capacity for self-love. When our children learn to love their "true self," as D. W. Winnicott defines it, they learn to accept their weaknesses alongside their strengths, their idiosyncrasies and needs, their victories together with their failures. They think about themselves with compassion, forgiveness, and trust, which allows them to attribute the same to others in their lives. They are free from the potentially toxic internal critic that can derail the best of intentions and impede their relationships. They feel whole just as they are—and all of this begins in the context of your relationship with your child.

Self-Esteem vs. Self-Acceptance

Many parents with whom I work confuse self-esteem and self-acceptance, and rightly so. The terms are bandied about and often used interchangeably. Whereas self-esteem refers specifically to how we measure or feel about ourselves, self-acceptance encompasses a deeper, more stable inner knowing of your own inherent value. When we're self-accepting, we're able to embrace *all* facets of ourselves—not just the positive, more "esteem-able" parts. As such, self-acceptance is unconditional, free of qualifications, and becomes the basis of self-knowledge. We can recognize our weaknesses and limitations, but this awareness in no way interferes with our ability to fully accept and love ourselves. It also means being able to work on self-growth by accepting faults, rather than judging them; it allows a person to be guided by a desire to improve or work on change.

When we love our children regardless of their interests, their personalities, how they move in the world, or, more concretely, their hairstyles or clothing choices, we convey the message that they are valued just as they are. We also convey our trust in them. This is different from helping them build self-esteem, which is tied to performance, accomplishments, achievements, and their competencies and skills. Parents are their children's first cheerleaders when it comes to acknowledging and praising the wonderful things our children can do—from clapping at their first step to applauding when they're handed their diploma. But even our unbridled enthusiasm can have limits and may send unintended messages to our children:

> What if they come in last in the track race?
> What if they get a C in math?
> What if they come up short and don't make the soccer team or the high school musical?

The danger is when children perceive these less-than-optimal outcomes as an indication that your love is tied to certain conditions. There are nuances here: we can validate our children's accomplishments and support their motivation to pursue goals, but not at the expense of undermining or weakening their sense of who they are. Sometimes our enthusiasm is so high (even if lovingly) it overtakes a child's ability to know if they are still loved if they do not do well at this sport or exam, act sweetly to everyone, or pursue an activity that you loved. Not making a sports team is not a failure that changes who they are, but it is if they equate making the team to being valued by their parent.

Even praising a child for an achievement can at times be interpreted by them as transactional: "If I do well at something, my parents will pay attention to me and love me more." The risk is that what begins to take shape in a child's mind is what I call the inner critic, a squeaky voice that makes a child second-guess themselves, judge themselves harshly, ignore their actual needs, and develop an overall distrust of or insecurity about themselves. This is the opposite of resilence. They define self-worth against how much praise or positive feedback they get from parents, teachers, and other adults. Similar to shame, this inner critic eats away at their positive sense of self. Most of us carry an inner critic within us, but as adults we have a better capacity to reframe that voice so that its impact is, at least, short-lived. However, children are more vulnerable to the effects of an inner critic; they may suffer from anxiety or become perfectionistic. They may shy away from challenges that they are not sure they will quickly succeed at and lack motivation for new experiences. When these reactions take root, they can interfere with a child's growth and development.

Malika is a great example of this. She is a highly verbal ten-year-old who has always done well at school. Teachers admire and praise her and so do her parents, grandparents, and many friends. She excels in school, loves math, and is labeled a "natural leader." But when she is faced with a new set of math challenges that she can't figure out right away, she clams up. She does not ask her teacher for help. Her stomach hurts and she asks not to go to school. Without praise for her frequent successes, she feels adrift and needs help to find her footing again.

She tells her mother, "I'm just stupid! I'll never get this!"

Her mother reminds her that she can and she will, but that it takes time. Malika remains silent and tears fill her eyes. Her mother begins to realize that all the praise has actually been detrimental to Malika's attitude toward herself. She thought she was good at everything and was not able to see that there is a process involved in learning. It is a lot of pressure for a child.

Malika's parents realize they need help to support her. Over time, her parents and grandparents learn to communicate a different message to Malika, one that brings more attention to the effort she puts in at school instead of the outcomes. They don't discuss grades anymore but note her progress. They ask her how she feels when she makes strides rather than telling her how great she is. Gradually and over time, Malika replaces her perfectionist attitude with one that is grounded in the belief that learning is a process that takes time and that mistakes—as well as less-than-stellar results—are part of that process. This attitude will become her own guide to success and help her build resilience to get through the next challenge. She won't be so stymied again as soon as she hits a hurdle in her learning. Instead, she begins to see learning as a step-by-step process with some steps forward and other ones back.

The very good news is that since you are your child's first and most important frame of reference for their own value and worth, you can reinforce your child's resistance to developing an inner critic and counteract it if it has already emerged. Regardless of their age, children will continue to look to you for confirmation that you see, love, and accept them for who they are. The challenge is ours as parents to work on our own biases and see our children for who they are.

That inner critic, which often stems from a lack of acceptance from parents, starts early and can last well into the adult years. A fifty-year-old mother told me that her highly critical and harsh mother finally complimented her on how well she is raising her children, alongside a challenging career. She said, "You have no idea how long I have waited for her to say something positive like this to me. She has never even acknowledged me as a good parent; all she had were criticisms of me. I have doubted myself for so long and needed this so, so badly, to hear her compliment me as a parent." This is from a woman with a highly successful career who is raising thriving children on her own; she is still waiting for approval from her mother and doubting herself in spite of her successes in life. Similarly, a father of teens once told me, "I was a late bloomer and became a father at forty-six. I spent most of my adult years trying to make my dad happy, waiting for him to be proud of me. It was never going to happen, but I still wanted it." We can help our children not be critical of themselves by learning to accept who they are and conveying it to them, even when understanding them is hard.

They May Have Their Own Schedule

What our children need can at times be confusing or hard to decipher. We can unknowingly overlook their needs or block ourselves from understanding them in other ways, too. Sometimes we get ahead of ourselves and impatiently expect our children to grow out of certain behaviors by a certain time, even though there can be reasons they have not. It's important to understand that any one child may be in their own process of two steps forward, one step back. We wish they would grow up and stop whining because they are "too old for that," be more responsible, be less needy of us, or take better care of their rooms. We may too easily label their behaviors as regressive instead of seeing that the child before us is communicating their needs—nearly always, there's a reason they are acting younger than you think they should be.

For example, three-year-old Adele had been toilet-trained since age two, loved rock-and-roll music like the Rolling Stones and the Beatles (just like her parents!) and requested that her parents put it on, and was beginning to read simple words in her favorite books. Her parents marveled at how "mature she is for her age."

When Adele insisted that she wanted a "big girl bed now!" they jumped at the chance and took the side off her crib. Finally, no more baby! Ty and his wife, Karolina, were ready to have only big kids at home. Ty admitted that he enjoyed his children more as they got older. So imagine their surprise when their seemingly mature Adele refused to stay in her bed, wandered the house in the middle of the night, and then insisted she wanted to be back in diapers. And so began a series of regressive behaviors. Adele used baby talk and asked for bottles, which she had not had in over a year. She began using her diaper instead of going on the toilet.

Ty and Karolina were highly rattled by the time they reached me.

"What happened? Adele was so independent and on her way out of babyhood, and now she is acting like a baby again!" exclaimed Ty, who seemed to be more obviously upset. Karolina was quiet but looking down into her lap and clasping her hands.

I suggested we sit down to figure out what was happening. The more we talked, the more the parents began to re-see Adele as her age—three. They admitted that they liked her "independent streak" and how "tough" she could act, and that they probably catered to it too much. They also seemed to realize they'd forgotten how little she was, given that her brother was close to five years older. I urged them to see her as the very young child she was, more baby than big.

Upon their return home, they offered to put the side back on her crib (and she slept again!). They let her pretend to be a baby and they rocked her and sang her lullabies. At bedtime, they returned to snuggling her like they had when she was younger. Ty was hesitant and wanted my reassurance that if they held and comforted Adele in this way, it wouldn't interfere with her wanting to grow up and that she would not always be a baby. I assured him that if they could accept that she had a baby side to her as well as a side that wanted to grow up and be big (both parts reside in every child), then she would settle in, feel safe again, and be eager to move forward. Dad needed hand-holding, too.

In a couple of weeks, Adele was back to her delightful and strong way of being. Her parents remembered how little she was, and she felt safe again to grow up. They admitted that babying her with snuggles and recalling stories from when she was a baby felt good. This is being attuned: her needs were to be little, even if Dad was ready for her not to be anymore. When they tuned in to her needs, she felt comforted and calmer. She grew more secure and in time showed them she could grow up.

I see this dynamic often when a child's regression upsets or worries a parent. Understandably, this kind of change can startle us. Our reaction can be something along the lines of, "What?! You know better than this! You are capable of much more." And while they may be capable of more, right now they are not. Our inclination can be to move in fast, get punitive or angry, and make consequences over their lacking the capabilities we know they possess. What this response negates is the reality that children and teenagers regress sometimes, which is another way they communicate their needs.

Seeing Your Child

Accepting your child also entails acknowledging—and not judging—their differences. As mentioned earlier in the book, our responses to our children include ones that are subtle and often unconscious. If we sense our child is different from us or their sibling, we may inadvertently compare or criticize: "Why can't you be more like your brother or sister?" We may do this outwardly and say it, or it can be a quieter voice within us, which children can still pick up on and absorb.

We may not really "get" the tween who likes to stay up late and sleep late into the day when we are a morning person. We may get frustrated and anxious when all they want to eat is white food—pasta with butter, mac and cheese, chicken tenders—when we are a family who loves spicy foods and prides ourselves on gourmet tastes. We may not understand how or why they like scary movies or loud music. But by learning to give that child space to be who they are, which means seeing them and trusting them, they learn that you are respecting their personal boundaries, their needs at the time, and what makes them comfortable and gives them pleasure. (Besides, most kids will outgrow the white-food phenomenon, though it may not happen on your watch.)

One story that feels quite timely is about a couple who were struggling to accept their child's nonconforming gender identity. Nicolette, whose sex was male when she was born with the name Nico, asked to be called Nicolette when she turned eight years old. I knew this family starting when Nicolette was a baby and observed how Maya and Juan had grown comfortable with Nicolette's enjoying dressing in skirts and dresses and wearing her long hair in ponytails and sometimes a bow. Though she identified as a boy at the time, Nicolette showed consistent interest in sharing activities associated with the female gender. She liked accompanying Maya when she got her nails done and asked Maya to buy her colorful barrettes for her long hair.

Maya and Juan had asked me to work with them and their child's school on helping Nicolette's classmates and the community be inclusive and accepting. Together, we discussed that whether Nicolette was transgender or testing out gender identities in a more fluid way, the important piece was that she felt respected and accepted. To my observation, when Nicolette identified as a boy, her parents let her be herself. Juan and Maya were comfortable with having Nicolette explore girl activities and dressing up in female clothes.

However, when Nicolette approached them about changing her name, Maya and Juan became unsettled and unsure of what to do. They were also on edge and arguing more as a couple.

With my encouragement, Juan and Maya sought out additional professional support beyond our work together—both as a couple and then as a family with Nicolette and her siblings. They loved their child—regardless of her gender identity—and as parents they knew they could get to a place beyond simply being tolerant and of evolving into full acceptance of who their child was. They also recognized that they needed to do work on themselves to get there. Over time, Juan and Maya came to realize that at the heart of this situation was their needing to let go of who they'd thought their child was or envisioned she would become one day. In working through their own worries and fears about Nicolette potentially facing a life they worried would be filled with pain and rejection, they were able to see their child, whom they knew and loved regardless of her gender identity.

In time and with intention to understand who their child was, Maya and Juan came to fully accept Nicolette and shifted to how they could support their child, who now identified as female, in what she needed to continue to grow into a loving, self-assured, and resilient person. Once Maya and Juan were able to connect fully to their love for their child, they let that love be their guide, their North Star, as they processed their own feelings through grief, confusion, worry, and ultimately acceptance and understanding.

As parents, we will encounter times that ask us to reevaluate what our preconceived ideas are about our children, and the subtle (or less-than-subtle), unspoken expectations we have for them. Becoming aware of our own biases and expectations can feel scary, but facing our own fears and discomfort means not getting in the way of supporting a child on their unique growth path. Every child has one. Every child needs a parent to walk alongside them on it.

Children's identities and personalities can also present more subtle challenges to our fully accepting them without conditions. Think of the child who loves to jump on the furniture and especially the living room couch. It drives you crazy. Your tendency is to say (or yell), "Why can't you ever stay still? You never listen. Just stop for once!" Instead, you do the work to understand who this child is: one who is in near-constant movement. You don't have to criticize or shame her for her constant need for movement, but you could set down a rule that there's no jumping on the couch and suggest that she create another place to move her body and jump. There are times when it is even harder for us to see what our children need or respect their way of being. Without intending to do so, we might correct them or try to control them when they are just being themselves. Often, these are qualities or habits your child has that are different from you or related to parts of yourself you do not like and wish they did not emulate. This can include habits of our children that just plain bother us; for example, the child who:

- Is hard to awaken in the morning, or who wakes up slowly and in a rotten mood
- Needs constant movement and has a hard time focusing
- Has very particular food preferences and refuses to eat other foods
- Prefers to stay home, and is hard to get outside, even on the sunniest of days
- Does not like to read books, ever
- Repeatedly tells you they are bored and there is nothing to do
- Has one good friend and insists they don't want to be with anyone else
- Counters any suggestion you make, even when they request help
- Gets anxious before social events and refuses to go to birthday parties, family gatherings, or school socials
- Is hesitant to try anything new, including clothes, food, or activities
- Stands back and observes for a long time before ever joining in, if they do join in
- Needs to be reminded over and over again to do any household task
- Complains incessantly and never seems satisfied
- Rarely says thank you and seems ungrateful

So, what is a parent to do when you have a child who is hard to understand, has habits that constantly frustrate you, or has aspects/ qualities you don't like? Begin by asking yourself why these habits bother you, as gaining insight into yourself can be the switch you need to accept who your child is. In the context of a supportive and loving relationship, understanding your child's behaviors or point of view can help soften your view of them and help you accept rather than bristle. And remember, don't take it personally.

Teaching Self-Care

One way that children grow to respect and accept themselves, especially as they get older and more capable, is by assuming responsibility for their health and well-being. Actively teaching our children self-care skills is foundational to their respecting themselves. It's never too early to show children how taking good care of themselves and tuning into their own needs will help ensure that they have the skills to manage future stressors in healthy and effective ways. Doing self-care activities together not only helps your child cultivate good, lifelong habits, it also helps your child become aware of what can recenter them during times of uncertainty or instability.

Self-care comes in many different forms, from daily habits of physical care to special occasions when a little boost is needed. Sometimes it means indulging in a favorite food, extra time on a favorite screen activity, or binge-watching a show, but more often it's about teaching (and modeling) behaviors that show children the implicit benefits of being tuned in to their bodies. Pride develops out of being able to take care of one's wellness needs, physical and emotional.

Taking care of their bodies starts when they are young with the routines you put in place for bathing, brushing teeth, hair care, and bedtime. These routines turn into their own self-care as they get older. Take the time to explain to your children how good health habits boost the immune system and protect against nasty invaders like viruses and bacteria or how good sleep helps the child grow. As I noted earlier, try not to make these kinds of instructions a lecture (no one likes to be lectured, so your child likely won't hear it), but it can be incorporated into dentist or doctor visits or other naturally occurring times.

Over time, with daily routines and your support, they will learn how to brush their teeth, wash their bodies and private parts, and take care of their hair. If they have special needs, such as eczema or other skin conditions, teaching them how to apply lotions or creams is part of caring for their needs. The same goes for using an inhaler if they have one, or other medical needs. Explain how important a good night's sleep is to how well their brain will function during the day and how much better we feel. When my children were little and sleep challenges arose, I would gently and with humor note how much they had grown in the mornings after nights when everyone slept. From my years of working with families and raising my own three children, it is clear to me that helping children develop good sleep habits is a crucial way we can support their physical, mental, and emotional health. The science unequivocally supports the importance of sleep to our lifelong wellness and well-being. Sleep supports growth and development, learning and regulation, immunity, and how well your child can interact, cope with adversity, and enjoy life. Sleep is a crucial foundation of their resilience.

When you teach them about self-care from a young age, children grow to take care of themselves with pride. As children approach puberty, increased attention to self-care, including books on bodily changes and in conversations with you and their pediatrician or adolescent medicine doctor or other trusted adults, can help them take responsibility for their bodies and decrease the potential for feelings of shame regarding physical changes. You can also discuss mood and emotional changes, as well as topics such as puberty and its associated changes and growth. In such open forums, children will feel more in control of the changes and better able to ask questions. Such discussion can also help mitigate worries and help your child and teen positively embrace their growing and developing self. You may also benefit from reviewing your own feelings about these topics or how they were communicated to you so that you can be aware and not let them interfere with talking to and supporting your child. The cultures, religion, family of origin, and communities we grow up in all provide messages about bodies, puberty, and sexuality that can impact how we feel and what we communicate to our children. Shame often accompanies these topics, and the more aware you become, the better you can be about communicating positive messages to your child.

During different stages of growing up, your child might push back on self- and bodily care, which is a way for them to test their autonomy ("Do I really have to shower today? So what if I smell?"), but eventually they will absorb—and use—this information. So putting the information out there, nonjudgmentally, is important even if your child is not yet ready to take care of themselves on their own or is old enough to do it but still hesitant.

Share Physical Activities

Part of physical care is movement. Incorporating shared movement with your child, whether younger or older, inside or out, can be a way to connect while developing healthy physical habits. We tend to run around with young children with an awareness of their need to move their bodies and become less focused on this need as children grow. Physical movement is good for developing lifelong healthy habits across all ages; mounting scientific data evidence shows the harm of being sedentary on our mental and physical health. The more we incorporate this as part of being with our children, the more likely they are to develop these lifelong habits.

Enjoying physical activities is also a time for connection. We can forget as our children get older how important this shared movement remains, and it is often a time when parents and children share mutual pleasures (e.g., we both enjoy biking, or playing tennis, or looking for birds). Similarly, these shared times are when your child may open up and talk, tell you what is on their mind—without your asking. This unexpected and intimate connection happens because we are not asking anything of our child, with no rules or judgment. We are together, in repetitive movement that allows a connection and a time for the parent to listen without making any demands. Even our quietest children can open up then. Think of tossing a ball or Frisbee back and forth, or taking a walk, side by side. In both cases, there is a rhythm, and an ease, and your child who otherwise shares little with you may find the comfort to tell you something about themselves, or muse on what is happening in their life, not because you asked but because you are in connection together.

Beyond the benefits of movement, spending time together shows your child that you enjoy being with them and value who they are. Depending on your child and what they enjoy, suggestions include:

- Walks together, in your neighborhood, to the grocery store, or in the local park
- Walking the dog
- Walking in the rain or taking a hike in the woods
- Bicycle rides
- Tossing a ball/Frisbee; kicking a soccer ball
- Playground time
- Backyard or in-home obstacle courses
- Mutually enjoyed games such as tennis, basketball, soccer, or Ping-Pong
- Raking, planting, weeding, and other yard work
- Training for a running race together
- Lifting weights or another shared exercise routine

Physical activity can also help your child make the connection between physical activity and its positive impact on the brain and the body: the more exercise, the better they feel, the stronger their body and mind, the easier it is to concentrate on school projects, completing homework, or a creative task of their choosing. It can be fun to explore the idea that when they move their bodies, they increase the amount of energy they have—and then can play even more. Movement begets more movement. Exercise with your child does not have to be elaborate and should not be rigid or rule bound—it can be as simple as taking a walk, riding bikes, stretching or doing yoga, or playing hide-and-seek or tag in the backyard. Helping your child build their awareness between physical activity and a sense of enjoyment lays down the foundation for later on, when they can rely on exercise to help manage stress, relieve anxiety, and move through tough moments.

If your child is into sports, support them, even if it is not a sport you would have chosen or even know much about. One mother noted, "I was a competitive long-distance runner, and I played softball, yet all my son wants to play is soccer, so I've pushed myself to learn the basic rules to show my interest. When I share even a little bit of knowledge, he is so excited that I care about what he is doing to practice his skills."

You don't have to be the coach or on the sidelines every game to show you care (although that may be something you enjoy). Support can be taking part in the carpool or asking about their practice when you sit down for dinner. One Little League season, my children and I volunteered to rake and prepare the fields after a long winter. This turned out to be great physical activity and a fun afternoon. In some communities, being part of organized activities involves many children. Yet a child (or parent) doesn't need to be part of organized athletics to emphasize the importance of creating a regular routine of physical self-care that maintains good health and balance. Daily movement as part of regular habits can take one of many forms.

Let Loose and Have Fun Together

We often think of giggling, playing, and having fun as what younger children do and overlook its importance throughout life. A healthy and balanced life includes fun and play; plus, it becomes a built-in way to counter stress. Getting silly, enjoying games, and creating activities that are playful and pleasurable shows children how to let off steam, starting at the youngest ages and continuing throughout life. Young children play without any help from us; they run, skip, build, pretend, create, follow their curiosities, and otherwise play on instinct. It is part of their very being. This does not have to go away, and I strongly believe it should not. The pleasures of play are an integral part of a balanced life, and this inner harmony promotes a sense of self-acceptance. Sharing joy and laughter with your child coveys a clear message that you enjoy being with them.

As a parent you can model and emphasize the importance of this kind of fun to further reinforce your child's inner sense of being a full person, including the playful part. The older children are and the more pressure they feel at school and other goal-oriented activities, the fewer opportunities there are to fall into unstructured or spontaneous play. Be sure to emphasize that playful, relaxing moments are important for everyone's well-being. Depending on their age and interests, this can include watching a movie together on popcorn nights at home, baking cookies or other desserts, creating scavenger hunts, playing family board or card games, and doing a large puzzle together over many days. It may be sharing moments of unleashed mutual laughter or inside family jokes together or deciding to put on some music, let loose, and dance! Play activities that bring shared connection and joy allow everyone to de-stress. You can help children make the connection between letting loose and doing something for the sheer thrill of it and the boost in positive feelings that comes after. These are not extras in their life; rather, they are essential. And when you are fully present and engaged having fun together, you not only reinforce the strength of your connection but also help build a resource they can turn to when you're not around. I see this in my college students as they make jewelry, spray-paint murals, or do other art activities and create with play dough and clay when midterms or finals roll around. It is important for young adults to know that balance must be in their lives for healthy development and to counter stressful times.

Spend Time Outside

We all know how spending time in the outdoors is good for us, but it also provides children with a channel for self-care. Spending time outdoors stimulates growth and development and connects us to nature. Being in natural environments is the first step in learning to take care of it. It also helps build our immune systems and provides another way to relax and ward off stress; being in nature improves health for children and adults alike.

Many cultures emphasize the importance of children spending time in fresh air—to avoid disease and improve overall good health. When I ran our toddler program outside throughout the first year of the pandemic, including a long, cold winter, I learned firsthand the value of helping children spend time in the elements—whether it be rain or snow, sleet, or whipping wind. One of my favorite memories from that year involved a group of two- and three-year-olds opening their mouths wide to catch the heavy rain on a chilly, soggy day, giggling with delight as the cold rain tapped against their faces. The adults were cold, but the children were filled with joy. Parents repeatedly reported how well their children slept on their outside days. I suggest embracing the seasons and getting to know your local area environment with your child. If you live in a city, spending time in the park and at playgrounds, exploring new neighborhoods with children of all ages, and finding new places to play can be great shared activities. If you live near a nature preserve or forest, take walks through the woods. Thanks to my spouse, who embraces nature, hiking, and being outside, a favorite activity of our boys was turning over logs in the woods (or any nearby park) to see what life was living underneath. Hikes together, whether children want to be part of planning and mapping them (especially as they get older) or simply going with you, provide a connection to nature and a sense of freedom (think of the pleasure and independence a child feels when they go ahead or lead the family on the trail). If you live near a body of water or beach, look for shells or other treasures; one of my most cherished memories is of searching for sea glass and washed-up driftwood on the shores of Lake Erie as a child. To this day, I walk with my eyes down on any beach, still looking for washed-up sea glass.

Perhaps your family is more adventurous and enjoys camping, snorkeling, or longer types of daylong hiking—any and all time spent in the great outdoors will help your child build a relationship to the natural world and build memories with you, and provide plenty of opportunities to problem-solve and get through mishaps (how to light the camp cooking fire when the wood is wet; how to navigate out on a new trail or what city bus to take to a favorite playground) and a love of the outdoors your child will enjoy and incorporate for the rest of their lives. As children move into their teen years, venturing outdoors with friends can be a way to find increased independence while being social.

The important message is that getting outside matters for your child's health and how they feel about themselves. Self-love includes connections to nature, and spending time outside does not have to be elaborate—your yard, a public garden, or a local park can all offer a chance to enjoy fresh air.

Volunteer to Help Others in Your Community

As mentioned in the last chapter, doing for others makes us feel good and has a positive effect on our overall health. Research findings suggest that people who are more secure and accepting of themselves also are more prone to give to others. It's a virtuous circle: helping others makes us feel good about ourselves and helps others at the same time. This sense of connection to others increases our sense of inner wholeness and self-love. It reminds us that we are part of a larger circle, a community.

When parents model these behaviors in their own lives and provide opportunities for children to join them, it instills habits of mind they can follow in their lives. We used to help fill the playground sandboxes in the spring for a community sand day, as a start for children when they were young. Doing local park days—from planting to raking—is another communal activity. Donating to local clothes drives or food banks is another way for children to get involved, as is writing letters to elders in a local nursing home. A family told me recently that when they heard about immigrant families moving to their area, their school-age children wanted to make welcome cards and drawings and put together welcome packages. Their children were excited to deliver the packages and got to play with some of the children when they delivered their homemade gifts. What does that teach a child? That they have much in common with the newly arrived families: all children like to play.

As children get older, new opportunities will arise and your child's school may have a structure for this—making holiday decorations for a local hospital or care center, for example, or organizing food drives for a local food pantry. You can also suggest altruistic activities explicitly, including:

- Sharing their resources—whether this is a snack for a friend who forgot theirs or donating their allowance some weeks to a cause they care about (such as animal organizations or climate change). A friend told me that when an oil spill occurred and one of their children saw that the marine life was dying, he asked if he could send money to help the animals. With some research they found an organization helping to clean the oil off ducks in the impacted area. He did extra work around the house to earn money and donated this to the cause. Each child has different interests; try to connect to what they care about.
- Giving of their time—volunteering at the pet shelter, joining a neighborhood cleanup crew, or staying after school to help tutor younger children brings its own rewards; children and teens gain great satisfaction out of giving in these ways.
- Helping a neighbor in need—perhaps an older person in the neighborhood is ill and can't get to the store. Offer to walk their dog, water plants, or shovel their snowy walk; you and your child can organize a neighborhood group to help.
- Showing empathy and compassion—just like you show your own child empathy and compassion when they are having a hard time, you can encourage them to extend that to their peers, sharing a kind word when someone gets hurt and offering to listen if a friend seems troubled. Even in good times, altruism can be modeled. A parent told me about their fourth grader, who has two classroom teachers, both of whom were pregnant. With the help of parents, the students organized a shared baby celebration and collected money for

a gift for each teacher. The children shared in the excitement of the teachers' expanding families.

Whether altruistic actions are organized or informal, ongoing or in the moment, as in helping a friend or someone in need, they give children and teenagers a meaningful opportunity to give to others, to experience themselves as kind, caring people, and reinforce that they are part of something larger than themselves.

Practice Gratitude

We can also help our children and teens build a sense of gratitude. In doing so, they can focus on what they have and be more accepting of who they are. Research has shown that these two constructs are strongly correlated with resilience and an overall optimistic outlook on life. A surge of new studies examining how cultivating gratitude can improve well-being demonstrates that it buffers against negative states and emotions. The research and its results are so robust they've resulted in evidence-based "gratitude interventions," some of which I have adapted below to try for yourself and with your children:

- Create a nightly ritual of expressing at least one thing you or your child are grateful for that day; you can use words like, "something I am happy about, glad that happened, or someone who helped me today is . . ."
- Write a list of qualities you like about yourself and you're grateful for. Develop a ritual for adding to the list. Write a list of qualities that are not perfect or that are a challenge and make you who you are. This is part of accepting all of you.
- Keep a list of items or people you and your family are grateful for; it can be daily or ongoing, where you keep adding to it.

- When children are older (and especially if your child likes to write), suggest they keep a personal gratitude journal where they can write about positive happenings and what they are grateful for in their lives.
- Write gratitude letters (younger children can draw pictures and dictate messages) to family members, friends, coaches, or teachers—people in your children's lives. These are thank-you letters that highlight ways, small or large, that someone has helped them. Let your child decide to whom they want to write.
- Establish a practice of helping your child write thank-you letters when grandparents, relatives, or friends give your child a gift or take them on a special outing. If not a letter, then a thank-you phone call is a good practice to establish.

These exercises may sound obvious and in many ways are simple. The reason I highlight them here is that the connection between expressing gratitude and resilience is clear and the practice of it can be readily incorporated so that it becomes part of their everyday way of life.

Mindfulness Practices

"Mindfulness" is a term that is written about and discussed frequently today, and I find it an important one worth exploring. Recently, I've been tying my work with children and parents more directly to mindfulness techniques. By this I mean asking parents to stay present in the moment and not focus on the anxiety of what a child's behavior today means for their future, whether that is next week or next year. I suggest exhaling and inhaling and having mantras to ground parents and slow them down when their worries are driving their need to act fast rather than thoughtfully figuring out what is driving a child's behavior. Mindfulness puts us in the moment, focused on the here and now, and increases awareness and the ability to reflect on our emotional states. Working more directly with mindful techniques has highlighted for me once again how developing self-compassion allows children (and parents) to recognize and accept their own feelings rather than constantly challenging and berating themselves to "be better," "do better," "do more," or somehow change who they are.

Mindfulness points to being in the moment, an awareness of the present, and a focus on the now. With the extensive evidence of increases in anxiety, depression, and overall stress for our youth as well as adults today, focusing on being present is a practice that can counter the stressors and weights children feel. Research highlights that mindfulness supports well-being, good health, and resilience. Slowing down is good for us. Equally important is that mindfulness is also positively associated with a stronger sense of self and self-acceptance. In their extensive research, psychology professors Ellen Langer and Shelley Carson of Harvard University show that "one of the simplest and most natural methods of reducing self-evaluation and replacing it with acceptance is to assume a mindset of mindfulness rather than mindlessness."

Langer and Carson define a mindful mindset as being able to view situations from multiple points of view and shift perspectives depending on the context. In contrast, mindlessness is "a state of rigidity in which one adheres to a single perspective and acts automatically," which includes pigeonholing experiences, behaviors, and people into rigid categories (for example, "I will never be good at math because I did poorly on that math test"). The danger of this for our children is that they fall into negative thinking rather than recognizing that negative feelings and experiences are one of many aspects of who they are. Based on techniques developed by Carson and Langer that I've adapted, consider the following suggestions to incorporate mindful self-acceptance into your relationship with your child and practice yourself.

Encourage and teach your child to:

- Actively notice new things in and around them (such as flowers in bloom or leaves changing in the fall), and, to note the surprises; this noticing the positives and change stimulates the habit of also exploring new and undiscovered aspects of the self.
- Think of themself as a "work in progress," emphasizing a growth mindset. Make mishaps and mistakes part of any process; this practice can counter the development of shame because messing up and not getting answers right away becomes the norm.
- Contemplate puzzles, ironies, and paradoxes, which help build up a tolerance for the many ambiguities and inconsistencies of life; think of this as "expect the unexpected" as a preparation for life.

Add humor and lightness (respectfully) to the situation, which allows for an immediate way to see a new or unexpected side of a situation . . . or themselves. This is part of my "keep it light" philosophy, which can be so helpful as we face and get through tough situations, all the while trying our best to convey to our children that what seems like an insurmountable moment may not be so heavy and dark. A more spiritual approach to mindfulness, which is being studied widely by neuroscientists, has shown that mindfulness meditative practices also support a nonjudgmental attitude toward the self. Psychology professor and director of the Center for Healthy Minds at University of Wisconsin–Madison Richard Davidson has done extensive studies on how simple meditation exercises like breath work can improve one's attitude toward oneself and others, boost mood and quell anxiety, and ameliorate overall well-being. I've increasingly incorporated simple meditative practices into my own life and work with children and adults and have observed visible shifts in mood and attitude. Mindful and meditative practices can help achieve a sense of agency within oneself, which is another aspect of self-acceptance. Below are suggested activities for yourself and with your children to try to do (or adapt) in a relaxed way outside of stressful moments, so they can add them as skills to their growing repertoire of resilience resources, especially as they get older:

- Together, take three breaths, slowly inhaling and exhaling. You model; they can follow. Then let them lead, and you follow. You can achieve a rhythm together. Enjoy your time together.
- Once in a while, try to eat a meal in silence, paying attention to the sensory experience of tasting and ingesting food. Depending on the ages of your children, you can do this for longer (or shorter) amounts of the meal. After, talk about what each of you discovered in the quiet, describing what it felt like.
- Sit quietly and do a short meditation. You can start with a three- or five-minute meditation (and lengthen with practice), using an app or on your own (set a timer). Use simple instructions to sit and focus on the present moment, such as "focus on your breath; if your mind wanders, don't resist; bring your attention back to the breath." Or "focus on your body, starting at the top of your head and moving down slowly, noting each physical body part; feel the chair or floor below you."

It may be obvious by now, but worth restating, that the challenge is greatest when there is a mismatch between our child and ourselves. I urge you to start with yourself as the next step in thinking through how to get to self-acceptance, without feeling shame about who you are, so you can raise a resilient child.

The You Factor

Accepting your child requires intentional effort and a deliberate honesty to see the child before you—not the child who is similar to or different from their sibling or you; not the child who reminds you of your mother or father or bossy older sibling; not the child who you wish them to be. It may mean shifting your perspective so that you look at your child not as one who is lacking in some way (not motivated enough; too reticent to enter new situations) or who you so badly want to be different from who they are (less reactive; more social; more affectionate; less clingy). It means being aware of your own biases, desires, and expectations for them, and how these can color the ways in which you see and judge your child. At times parents report to me that they are ashamed of facing their biases or preconceived expectations. I encourage you to accept that we all have these; they are a natural part of who we are and what we bring to being parents. The more aware we become of these biases, the more clearly we are able to see each of our children.

Children read our intentions and tone for truth, so being genuine matters; it's what makes them feel that you have an authentic connection to them. Some of our comments about our children may seem innocuous and come from a place of love and kindness but may be heard differently by your child. You love that your son reminds you of your dad, who was such a great athlete, for example. You tell him that. But when you also recall times that your dad was overly harsh with you and your siblings, your son hears that, too. In his ten-year-old mind, he is like your father in all ways, and he believes that when you, the father he admires and adores, look at him, all you see is your own dad, the good coupled with the bad. The risk is that he takes this in and fears the bad parts of your father and develops his own inner critic and shameful feelings about himself.

When you make an offhand comment to your thirteen-year-old daughter about not eating too much at dinner, you may not be aware of how it lands: that you will only love her if she's thin. Audrey, a mom in one of my longtime parent groups, brought up how Sadie, her sixteen-year-old daughter, called her out for commenting when she lost weight after being away.

The mom recalls, "I told her she looked great! She'd come home from an outdoor adventure trip and had lost a lot of her teen chubbiness. I was excited for her to go back to school looking good. But she turned on me, saying, 'Mom, that's my body, not yours! I don't like when you speak about my appearance!' And here I was just trying to be complimentary."

This mother was clearly surprised by the reaction and upset with her daughter. After all, she had meant no harm.

When I asked Audrey about her own experience with her appearance, she shared a story from when she returned from college having gained weight her freshman year. Then, over the summer, she worked two different waitressing jobs and lost the fifteen pounds she'd gained. One evening, her mother, whom she described as "hard to please," turned to her, clearly happy, and said, "You're back to being my daughter again." Teenager Audrey was taken aback.

"I just felt so ashamed. And enraged. At the time I was not sure why I was so angry, but I was." Audrey explained, "Clearly, she loved me best when I met her narrow standards." Further discussion brought out an underlying focus on food and running comments on weight, looks, or health in her house growing up. This is a common phenomenon for many families from a variety of cultures (mine included).

There were a lot of knowing nods that day in the parenting group. Audrey, without ever being aware, was mimicking her own mother's attitude toward weight and appearance with her own daughter now; she was also unknowingly letting it interfere with seeing her daughter.

"I really don't care what Sadie looks like—I just want her to feel loved in a way that I did not. I was always being judged."

When we discussed that the way to not-judge her own child could be to not comment at all, she took note. "Maybe I need to let her tell me how she feels about herself, and then I can validate her."

Another mother in the group shared, "I was the only curvy one in the family. My two sisters and mom prided themselves on being slim—small hips and breasts. My mom would say, 'Oh, you take after your dad's side of the family,' and it wasn't a compliment."

One by one, they realized how much judgment there had been in each of their families, without having had much awareness of it. The judgments had often been about weight and beauty, but it also raised their awareness about academic performance and other pressures: "Who was smart was a big focus in my house"; "Being a top athlete also got noticed by my parents, and I never was that." Awareness is the first step in avoiding having these pieces we bring with us from childhood get in the way of being able to see and accept our children.

How we speak to our children may echo our own internal self-talk, especially the negative kind. Parents who unintentionally criticize or judge their children often do so from their own inner critic—that voice within them that never seems satisfied.

So how do we gain awareness and become less harsh critics of ourselves and thereby our children?

1. Start by recognizing when it is happening. Ask yourself: Am I being judgmental of myself? Am I having negative thoughts about myself or my child (she will never listen; he is so lazy; I'm a terrible parent)?

2. Ask yourself if you are criticizing your child, whether directly or offhandedly: "You never listen; what's wrong

with you?"; "Why are you so mean to me?"; "Can't you just stop moving so much?"

3. Stop and notice. Don't beat yourself up for your thoughts or critiques. Sit with them. Noticing brings these thoughts to awareness, a critical step and required before you can work toward change. Note your ability to catch the thought and inhibit it.

4. Do all you can to stop yourself from feeling bad about having these thoughts. They are tied to experiences in the past. Negative thoughts do not magically appear; they are rooted somewhere. There is a backstory, even if you are not aware of what that is just yet. The deeper work would be to uncover the backstory, but stopping and becoming aware as a first step matters.

5. Ask yourself: What makes me think there is a good and bad way to do this? Whose standards am I comparing myself (or my child) to?

Many parents (particularly but not exclusively mothers) get upset when a visiting relative comments on their way of interacting with their child—with such remarks as "You should discipline him"; "You give her too much freedom"; "I would never let my teenager speak to me like that." Even if their intentions were benign, their comment gets under your skin, and you start to question the decisions you are making as a parent. You argue with your partner over it. Try to catch yourself before you get more upset. Rather than letting this comment push you into a negative spiral, ask yourself why this comment is so upsetting to you. Who doubted you when you were a child? Whose voice does this remind you of? The more you can locate a source of the negative thoughts and associations, the less power the thoughts will have over you. But even if digging deeper does not help you identify the cause of the thoughts, allow yourself to calmly say,

"It is okay that I have these thoughts. I can become aware and not act from them. I don't have to put myself (or my child) down."

The process to stop self-critical thoughts or judgment of your child will take time. When you note a pattern (repeatedly seeing your child as lazy or unmotivated; wishing they were more social; thinking your child hates you and only wants their other parent; or always feeling negative in response to other people's comments), stop for a moment and ask yourself where those thoughts are coming from.

This kind of self-reflection can increase your awareness and help you move to a better place of kindness toward yourself, and ultimately toward your child. And yet you will make these criticisms of your child at times. The key is catching yourself, noting the negativity, and going back to your child to repair. You can say, "I know I blamed you for not taking care to finish your tasks around the house. I called you lazy. That was not nice, and I should not have said that. I apologize." Then see if you can help them get their tasks done. This action is a coming together that shows you are truly sorry. Mending with an apology can reconnect the two of you, even if it takes your child some time to fully accept your apology. Give them the space they need. This shows your child how to own their mistakes, that you still love them even if what you said was harsh, and that even the parent they trust and love is not perfect.

The biggest gift we can give our children is a genuine and radical acceptance of who they are, which means accepting all of their many pieces—positive, negative, strengths, and flaws. This means, too, helping them grow in their own awareness of who they are, what they require to stay balanced, and how to ask for help when they are in need. A primary factor in supporting a child to become their best, authentic self is you, the parent or other special adult in the child's life. As we've discussed throughout *Raising Resilience*, your child looks to you for comfort and safety, limits and recognition. Through the very nature of your relationship, its containing and anchoring, you offer a powerful path to resilience.

You have your own parallel journey to self-acceptance. When you are able to know yourself deeply, become aware of your own needs and desires, you are in a better position to fully accept yourself—your flaws and insecurities alongside your strengths and virtues. You are more capable of seeing your child as a separate person, someone who deserves to be seen and loved for who they are, no strings attached. In extending this love, your child will feel it, absorb it, and grow into the unique and independent individual they are meant to be. That is what I mean by raising resilience.

REFLECTIVE QUESTIONS

As parents we can be unaware of our own ways of thinking or experiences that might interfere with our view of our child and how we relate to them. Bringing these obstacles to awareness can help us see our children more fully through a clearer lens and learn to celebrate them as the people they are meant to be. This reflection, shedding biases and increasing self-awareness, is something that needs to be cultivated. Be patient with yourself as you step through this process.

- When you were a child, did you feel seen and accepted for who you were? Who embraced you like this? If you did not experience being accepted, think about what that was like for you, and what you wish had been different.
- Do you recall ever being misunderstood as a child? Think of when this was and how it felt to you.
- Did you ever feel you had to act a certain way or decide on specific choices to make your parents or other adults happy?
- What do you wish adults had understood about you that they did not? How would this have made you feel differently as a child? How do you think it would impact you now as an adult?
- Do you remember times when a parent or other adult reacted

by withholding affection or love or scolding you because you didn't behave in a certain way or failed to meet their expectations of how they thought you should be? What was that like for you?

- Did you receive messages that you were not a likeable or good person, or that adults did not like the way you acted or moved in the world? When did this happen and what do you recall from it?
- Do you recall being punished or shamed for not meeting the expectations of adults? When did this happen and how did you react?
- Are you aware of your own inner critic, the piece that is hardest on yourself? When do you hear it, and whose voice do you hear criticizing you? How can you respond to counter that negative voice?
- What expectations did adults have for you, and were they reasonable or hard to fulfill?
- Do you catch yourself falling into "glass-half-empty thinking"? When does this happen and what is it focused on?
- How open are you to shifting your own perspective and cultivating more positive emotions? What gets in your way of change?
- Do you recall a parent or other adult who listened to you without judgment or criticism? Recall a time this happened, who it was, and how it made you feel.
- Do you practice self-compassion? What do you do to be kind to yourself when you mess up?
- Do your current expectations for your child help or get in the way of truly accepting this child? What can you do to better accept who they are?
- Where do your expectations come from? Whose voice guides you? Are your expectations for your child reasonable?
- How might you shift your expectations to better understand and accept this child?

A Final Note

At the same time that I was writing this book, I was helping a young friend prepare to become a mother; one of life's greatest and most transformative transitions for a person happens in becoming a parent. I watched as she prepared for the arrival of her first baby, and as she and her partner got ready to take on this new life-shifting role as parents, after having left their home and arrived in a new country. I watched them fumble, make their way, and get into their rhythms with this new baby. What I mostly marveled at was the incredible joys they were experiencing, the shared wonders of the new baby, and the moments of mutual joy together as he smiled and then laughed, cooed, babbled, and looked for them, quickly growing in his trust that they will meet his needs. Their connection to their child was palpable, and I knew that the love was sowing the seeds of safety, security, trust, and the ability to go out into the world.

When we give our children a loving base to help them face life in all its beauty and complications, let them feel loved, and teach them how to give love, they become like sturdy trees with roots deep and wide. They are then able to grow strong within themselves and reach toward their larger community and world. They will feel inspired to contribute to that world and capable of experiencing the joys and wonders of life. Of course, they will encounter uncertain times, challenges, and disappointments, some of which will bring them surprising pleasures, while others will feel only like hardship and pain. But whatever the event or its outcome, their roots will remain resilient, enabling them to adapt and continue to grow. Their resilience first takes root within their relationship with us. It is our love, kindness, and care that ground and strengthen the roots, let them grow and flower. Raising a child from baby to adult is in itself a testament to resilience—ours and theirs—and its greatest measure is when they want to come back home even after they are out in the world more fully.

Being a parent is a challenge and a joy, filled with pleasures and mysteries, expectations and unknowns. And yet we all can turn to the wisdom of what has come before and the compilation of what we know from years of science and practice and work with families and children. What I have aimed to unpack in this book is what all children need to become independent and thrive, to love and accept themselves and give caringly to others. This outcome stems directly from the containing and anchoring you provide through your relationship. But please keep in mind that you can't do it alone, so try to find like-minded people in relatives, neighbors, mentors, clergy, community residents, or friends to support you along the way. Turn to professionals when you need them. Be forgiving of yourself and love your child for who they are. Take life one step at a time and know in your heart you are always well intentioned. Two steps forward and one step back is a good way to approach being a parent and understanding your child. You've got this. You have the strength to do it. Enjoy the journey and keep your sense of humor. It helps!

Acknowledgments

This is a book about relationships, the context in which development and life unfolds. Relationships are what sustained me through the writing of *Raising Resilience*. I am filled with gratitude for the many people with whom I get to be in relationships, some in the realm of my work life, others in my personal life, many of you in both.

My book agent, Yfat Reiss Gendell, and her assistant, Ashley Napier, of YRG Partners, for your guidance, support, cheerleading, and your motivation and efforts to land this book in the place it needed to be. The entire team at HarperCollins who believe in this book and my work, you understood right away that uncertainty is the one certain piece of life. My editors, Karen Rinaldi and Kirby Sandmeyer, took over the manuscript midstream with dedication to its success and recognized how badly the world needs this book. I am so thankful you did. To the marketing team and everyone involved in getting this out to readers, I am grateful.

A huge shout-out to my friend and collaborator Billie Fitzpatrick. We began on the topic—uncertainty—back in 2016, and then the world changed, and you walked with me and heard my ideas about parenting, trauma, daily life challenges, and the unknown. And both of our lives changed—love and loss, our children moving into the young adult years, and the pandemic. This journey of relationships and uncertain times and so many conversations and your skill, especially when our editorial team changed, has led to this book. Thank you is hardly enough.

Uncertainty is countered by the longevity of the deep bonds of many lifelong friendships. Some go back over fifty years—Barbara Tidwell Mahovlic, Heidi Gorovitz Robertson, Miriam Reshotko, Andrea Carmosino, Rassoul Teimouri, my cousin Haley Venn—and others not quite as long—my sister-in-law, Dulce Carrillo. Laura Bennett Murphy, who is not only with me through thick and thin, but she is also an advisor on this book and helped me think through detailed aspects of what children need during traumatic times and when handling daily hard moments. You are a gift in my life, for laughter, love, and tears, and the kind of friendship I wish for every child and parent to have in theirs. Nim Tottenham, friend and advisor on this book, with whom I have shared my personal and professional life for nearly thirty years, you are always at the ready to discuss neurodevelopmental processes, recommend journal articles to answer questions about brain development (often the same question multiple times), and as my research collaborator. My understanding of these areas keeps growing because of you.

No matter how young or old we are, I've learned we enter new relationships with potential to bring excitement and care to our lives. Whether we met as adults recently or in our early parenting or career parts of life, you have been by my side, through ups and downs, illnesses and loss, joys and connection. I'm grateful for each of you—Sandra Pinnavaia, Lisa Tiersten, Marci Klein, Michele Berdy, and Yvonne Smith. To Jamiyla Chisholm, who has been a loyal support through this writing process and as a writer herself knew how hard it could get. To Sarah Hahn-Burke, who stepped in as a professional support and personally as a friend. And to Mauricio Cifuentes, who keeps listening to my journey and encouraged my vision for years.

I am indebted to the multitude of moms, dads, grandparents, and caregivers who openly share their lives and children (including entire extended families) with me. Whether on a day-to-day basis at the center, or over time as your children grow into teens and adults, or in a one-on-one meeting or ongoing (for years!) parent groups and relationships, I am appreciative for every one of you. You teach me with your openness and vulnerability about who you are, what drives you, your relationships and history, and your motivation to understand how to be that parent you envision. Thanks for entrusting me with your dreams, joys, visions, shortfalls, fears, and worries.

A special recognition (with permission) to the Friday parent group that started back in the aughts: Felicia, Caroline, Emily, Liz, Susie, Alise, Diana, Ji, Seema, Allison, Lisa, Beryl, Marie, Amy, and others. I continually learn more from your willingness to embrace faults and forgive yourselves, to staying open to the discovery of who your child is and who you are and wish to be, from caring for your children and now teens and college-age young adults and your ailing parents and life's ongoing transitions. I am indebted to you as mothers, fabulous women, and friends.

I have much appreciation for Barnard College and the psychology department that has been my faculty home since 1995, where I have the distinct privilege to teach, advise, and mentor bright and bold Barnard (and Columbia) students, and where I conduct research aimed to better understand children and parents, and for my colleagues for three decades, Peter Balsam, Rae Silver, Robert Remez, and Sue Sacks. I am grateful to the many students I have the luxury to know through courses I teach, the center, and as advisees. You keep me informed about what it's like to be a young adult today, let me in on your changing world, and make me a better teacher/mentor with your questions, wide-open eyes, critical views, and wonderings. Thank you for including me in your lives, even long after you graduate.

To those I share my life with nearly every single day at the Barnard Toddler Center, my work-family who dig in deep together to give children and parents what they need. The teachers, staff, grounds crew, facilities people, security, and more over many years. We did it through the depths of the pandemic and now in a magical new space.

This includes our current team—Hannah Corrie, Alison Itzkowitz, Robin Otton, Ketaki Krishnan, Carly Stein, Leslie Perrell, Ayomide Tikare, and Nicole Gavrilova. To Andrea Fields, who stepped in this year while I wrote this book and treasures the research and applications aspect of the Toddler Center as much as I do. And to the many past staff members whose friendships I value long after you are here, Sabrina, Karina, and Jenna amongst them.

Michelle, Debbie, Oliver, Juan, and others who are loyal in their maintenance and daily upkeep of our center—even throughout pre-vaccine COVID—a huge thank-you. We would not be functioning at this high level for students and the community, or carrying out research if it were not for all of you.

And particularly to Alison Davis, who was new to Barnard just before the pandemic. Together we successfully ran programs for children, for parents, for college students through the entire pandemic and beyond. I learned how much uncertainty we could face and get through and that it requires more flexibility and adjustment than I knew. I'm grateful to your willingness to jump into the unknown together, including toddler programs outside through cold winters and for toddlers online. We may have thought it to be impossible, but we did it and did it well. It must go back to our University of Michigan roots!

Amy Schumer, I am beyond grateful for your nominating yourself to write the foreword in the midst of all you do, and for letting me into your life as a parent, a woman, an advocate for justice, and more. Thank you.

Natacha, for being part of our family and home life and helping with the many tasks that need to be done but I cannot get to.

To my brothers, Joe and Sam, who've always been by my side (towering over me with your height) and who taught me that relationships filled with needling and fighting and fun as kids turn into laughter and humor and ridiculous memes sent back and forth as adults. Every time someone comments on how lucky I am to have brothers I am so close to, I smile. I know that no matter where our parents are now that they are not in this world, we have each other and each other's back. That's an important lesson that was given to us years ago—our sibling battles are our own, and so are our relationships and care for each either—love you both and look forward to more travels together. It is fine that we root for different sports teams, #MGoBlue.

To my newest family members, Leleyscka, Tony, and baby Ethan, welcome. Watching you become parents while living in my home and being greeted by Ethan's joyous smile is a privilege. I know that new relationships come in life, but I did not know how readily I would be able to welcome new family; you have made that easy.

My parents, to whom I dedicated this book and whose life lessons are embedded in who I am and the work I do, each gave me something that I hope shines through in this book. My mother was a trailblazer who had to be strong in many ways, having a professional career before women were supposed to while also being a mother; my role model for commitment, passion, and rolling up your sleeves to make life better and advocate for those without voice. My father, my anchor and calm; a model for being real in the world—seeing the good, recognizing the bad, incorporating it, and moving on. Aiming to create better and not accepting the status quo as okay; a true moral compass of love, kindness, humanity, and being true to yourself. He taught me what deep, caring connection and unconditional love is. I know to listen, look, ponder, and not be afraid, as long as I stay true to myself, because he saw and understood me.

And to my family, who genuinely make me who I am and push me to be better (even when I don't care to be), to know myself, and to be authentic in this world. My children, Elam, Aaron, and Jesse, you turned me into Mom; you teach me so much about people and sincerity and owning my own stuff and, simply stated, bring tons of joy. I now get to watch you each make your own pathways as young adults. I know how fortunate I am to have the three of you.

My husband, Kenny, for being there, helping me get through rough spots, introducing me to new horizons and journeys as our relationship and lives together deepen over time; for reminding me of humor when I most need it; for our shared laughter and care. I love you.

Parenting Reminders for Raising Resilience in Daily Life

1. **Mantras are grounding**: I begin with this because raising children starts with you, the parent. The key to being that "good-enough" parent is to find ways to keep yourself centered, as best you can. There will be times when you get pulled into your child's or teen's emotional spiral or orbit. It is not a place you want to be. Note what is happening. Regain your balance. Your steadiness will help steady them. Think of a mantra fast and re-ground yourself. Here are some possible mantras to use:

   "I am the adult here."

   "She is not out to get me; this is just one moment in time."

   "This won't be forever; he's just a little person."

   "I must keep myself centered; my child needs me."

   By reminding yourself that you are okay, that you can handle this, and by bringing yourself back to a calmer here and now, you will be able to turn to your child in a clear, stabilizing way. They need us to stay in our calmer, more grounded lane and stay out of theirs. Then we can connect with intention and care and help them feel safe again.

2. **Be reasonable, as best you can**: When you are reasonable, including in the most challenging moments, you are giving your child a model for life. Interactions such as speaking to them, putting up limits, and giving them room to ask/push back within reason teaches them how to treat other people with respect. When you are harsh with your child, they learn to use the same tactics to get what they want

or need. You are their role model, and they see, feel, and absorb your actions.

3. **Let your child know you believe in them**: When you show you trust they can do something, they learn to trust themselves even when it's difficult. This means taking a step back at times and watching and asking yourself, "Can my child handle this? Is her frustration okay? Do I trust her to figure this out?" Giving them space to try to solve a problem one way or another and use their own ideas and resources gives children a chance to test themselves and gain confidence to try something again. This is true in many situations—from climbing at the playground, to buttoning their own shirt, to completing a chemistry problem set. Knowing that you are on the sidelines, ready to assist if they ask for your help, gives them the security they need to try.

4. **Err on the side of kindness, even in their worst moments**: When children are having a hard time, screaming, stomping, or being rude and talking back, your reflex may be to yell back, scold, try to control, or shame them. Instead, staying steady with kindness will go further. Sending the message, "I am here for you always, even when you fall apart," reminds them that you care, that they are not alone. If you model kindness and compassion, then they learn to treat others the same way. You may first need to take a slow, deep breath to steady yourself, to figure out how to connect to your child and what limit you want to set up.

5. **Apologize, repair, and reconnect**: No one is perfect, nor should you strive to be. Relationships are about connection and trust, and at times disruptions and disconnections that feel uncomfortable for you and your child. This natural part of a relationship can be scary for a child, even for a teenager. Engaging in a repair after a blowup or other less-than-ideal interaction with a genuine apology and ac-

knowledgment of your part in it is key; it brings the two of you back to connection. Be honest and direct:

"I'm sorry I yelled like that."

"I apologize. I should not have done that."

"I'm sorry I didn't listen to you earlier."

Taking responsibility to make the repair brings relief to your child and provides a model of how to deal with anger and disruptions in other relationships in their lives, including with friends or romantic partners. Even if your child is not ready to accept an apology, your beginning the process to reconnect is still reparative. Be open to their coming back to you when they are ready. Children need the repair and reconnection to buffer them from owning the disruption as their fault and problem, which turns into shame.

6. **Be your child's buffer and keep anxiety at bay**: Stress and bad things will happen. Traumatic events may occur. In the everyday building of your relationship with your child and teen, you are building the buffer for when these hardships come their way. By knowing you will be there for them and that you will try to stay focused on calming the crisis and getting to safety with them, a child does not have to absorb the enormity of a highly charged or frightening situation. When crises occur, your ability to keep your own anxiety and fear in check will let you offer support and guidance in a steady way, enabling your child to learn to regulate on their own as they grow up. This is a way to protect them from long-term negative impacts of stress, trauma, or life's many challenges.

7. **Boredom is a gift**: In a busy, high-tech, multitasking, stimulus-overloaded world, boredom is a gift. Embrace it for your children. Insist on it for your teens. Downtime is good. It is in these unstructured, low-demand moments that each person has time to think, ponder, imagine, wonder, nurture curiosity, problem-solve, or

simply sit back, stare, and relax. Boredom brings calm. As a step on the path toward independence, boredom gives your child the time to sit with their thoughts, listen to their breathing, think about what they want to do next, and overall be comfortable being with themselves and their own ideas. You can help your child reframe boredom. Being bored is not "doing nothing"; it's a valuable time to de-stress, be creative, gain perspective, and practice mindfulness. Think of these moments as an opportunity to let the mind wander. Looking out a window at the rain falling, or staring quietly into space, counters the fast-paced, instant gratification, demanding life that most of our children experience today.

8. **Getting through tantrums** is easier once you understand what they are and learn not to take them personally. Your child is not out to get you (even when it feels that way); they are truly in a heated state and need your help. A child has a right to be upset, but that can be a challenge if their brain cannot yet handle strong emotions. Tantrums happen at all ages, from a melting-down toddler to a tween or teen screaming how much they hate you. When intense, negative emotions (such as anger, frustration, and disappointment) arise, their brain capacity gets overloaded, like a waterfall when the water goes over the edge and ferociously tumbles down. That kind of full-on overwhelmed state is scary for your child. What to do to help during such intensity? Start with yourself, then your child:

   - First, settle and ground yourself, exhale, and use a verbal reminder or mantra—"I am the adult; I can handle this"—to steady yourself.
   - Remind yourself this is not personal, that emotions have taken over. Let go of the precipitating cause; let go of your own anger.
   - Next, move in closer. Note what is happening to orient

them using a calm, clear voice—no rationalizing, punishing, shaming, or blaming. The focus is on bringing down their arousal.

- Label what is happening: "You are so mad about that!"
- Orient them by reminding them that you are present and will keep them safe.
- When you feel a connection, start to breathe with them; either talk them through one or two breaths or breathe on your own. They will feel your breathing, so take deep—even exaggerated—breaths.
- When your child begins to calm, change the environment, go for a walk, or shoot some basketballs. Or sit and hold them, letting them know you are there for them.

Learning to handle an explosive moment takes time and is harder for some children than others. Similarly, as a parent, you will need to work on yourself and your reaction so you can help your child. The human brain takes a long time to learn to handle these emotions, and you are the one helping them learn, their partner.

9. **Routines matter**: Transitions are a sticky point for many children. Even for adults. They destabilize us and cause stress. At heart, we tend to like what we know; it is predictable and familiar. Home to school. Playing to dinnertime. Social media to homework. Reading time to math instruction. These are all transitional moments as we move from what we are doing now to something next (and maybe even new).

Every day is filled with multiple transitions for all of us, forcing us to face a bit of uncertainty each time. Some children will have a harder time than others when it comes to handling the shift. This is when routines matter, especially for anything done regularly. A mostly set routine makes the transition more predictable, provides a sense of control (I know what comes next; I know what is expected; I can do this), and helps a child move toward being more independent. If they hang their coat on the same hook every day, eventually they can do it on their own. Same with a place for homework following their afternoon snack, or clothes laid out to facilitate dressing in the morning. The more routines that are in place, the steadier people feel. The daily routines that provide stability are also practice for larger transitions, whether they are planned (a new house; a new school; first after-school job) or unexpected (dislocation due to flooding or fire; death of a loved one). Think of routines as the counter to transitions and be gentle in guiding your children through them. Repeated reminders are needed.

10. **Mealtimes matter**: They are family routines and times for connection. Mealtimes with young children are not always fun. With teens, it may be hard to cut out the space to have meals together, but do your best to find the time; they matter. Meals are part of routines, and connection happens when you come together and break bread as a family. In a busy family, try to set aside some dinners or weekend lunches each week so that you can all gather together. Make meals about the social aspect, not the food. Even your youngest children can help in cooking, serving, and being able to help themselves from a buffet spread on the table (scooping their own rice or broccoli adds to their desire to eat). As children get older, they can help plan meals and cook. These are life skills. Children like routines, and that includes sitting at a table, often in the same chair and place each night. While you eat, chat about the day and share funny moments that happened. Children talk most when they are not questioned directly, so keep it open and conversational, as in, "I saw the first spring flowers today" or "Can you guess who I ran into at the store on my way

home?!" "Did anyone have something happen today that was good, bad, or surprising?" It helps to have clear guidelines for expectations (no phones or devices at the table, for example; we stay at the table to eat). Leave out criticism or judgment so that food and meals are associated with positive times together.

11. **Drop perfection and become a better parent**: I don't know when perfection became an aim of parents, but I do know it is not attainable. Being a good-enough parent is the ideal for children; it shows your humanness and vulnerabilities, a good model for children. Through their relationship with you, children learn about reality, which means sometimes doing things well, sometimes not. Sometimes being happy, sometimes not. Sometimes pleasing others, sometimes not. Reality is learning to handle the imperfect moments that can be done safely in connection with a parent or another trusted caregiver. Your child must see the imperfections of the people they rely on to know that being less than perfect is human; then they don't have to fear their mishaps and can face up to their own vulnerabilities and imperfections, without shame. The true deep learning about self, about who to depend on and how relationships work, comes from admitting and working with such imperfections. Be forgiving of yourself. Real life is messy, and it is our role as parents to help children know that.

12. **Negative feelings are a must**: When we help our children sit with and handle negative emotions, we are extending them a powerful tool for resilience. Learning to regulate emotions is the secret to building the resilience to handle life. When a child experiences negative emotions and is not ridiculed or punished for their emotions, then they learn how to feel, accept, face, and get through them. But as a parent it can be hard to allow a child to "be upset." If you feel

your job is to make your child happy, then negative emotions in your child will be harder to handle. You may think you have failed as a parent. Instead, when you help a child accept these hard feelings, know that all feelings are normal and that they are loved regardless of how they feel, then they can learn to have all emotions, process them, and eventually move forward again.

13. **Listen to and hear what they have to say:** Children, no matter their age, want to be heard. More than almost anything else, they need us to listen to what they have to say, no phone in hand. Even when what they are telling you sounds odd, or in need of a response, remember that your child's desire is to talk without being judged or even being helped at that moment. Often, it is not about problem-solving; that can come later. For now, they want to talk or vent, and to be heard. Give them the space to do so. At times, our inclination is to correct and find solutions for our children. It turns them off. They get mad. They shut down. Instead, try taking a deep breath, stepping back, pausing, and listening to your child. Hear them out. Listen to their stories, their interpretations of what is happening, their musings on life. Active listening builds trust. And when you start this practice when they are young (putting your phone away, hearing them), then they tend to continue to open up as they get older. When children feel like they will be corrected or scolded or judged when they tell you what they did, they won't talk. Instead, be their sounding board. Venting sessions, often after school or near bedtime, allow your child to complain and let out emotions, feeling safe with you.

14. **Siblings:** "If I didn't love you, I'd hate you" is a line from a Squeeze song, but it's an apt adage for sibling rivalry. Siblings love; they hate. As long as they return to love at some point after (which most often they do), then the conflicts and rivalry between them can form a healthy part of the texture of their relationship. Siblings share the

most important person or people in their lives: parents. In my first book, *How Toddlers Thrive*, I called sibling relationships a Lab for Life and a safe place to work out conflict; learn to negotiate, disconnect, and reconnect; have someone you share life with—joys, pleasures, and hard stuff. It is a place where children find their voice and learn to give and take. When parents can step back and give their offspring the room to have their conflicts, deal with them, and find ways to move on or take breaks, then we are giving our children lifelong skills alongside a lifelong bond. We want them to have each other for life without the parents in the middle. The only way they get there is if parents stop trying to lay down rules and get involved in conflicts. I find that siblings repair even after they have said the meanest things to each other. Hours (or minutes) later, they can be playing and laughing again. Resist getting involved or inserting yourself, and instead, set some basic ground rules, depending on what your limits are, such as:

- "When you keep hurting each other, it is time to take a break apart."
- "When the screaming and fighting go on and on, you'll have to separate and find different places to play."

Make sure the rules are applied equally to all siblings, which means staying neutral on your part and not taking sides (not always easy to do). Otherwise, do your best to stay out of it.

15. **Know thyself—and reflect on your past:** Being a parent means bringing our full selves into a deeply intimate relationship with our children. Knowing yourself and being open to learning more about yourself will help you as a parent. You may still be processing negative experiences from your childhood or after. You may want to replicate or actively avoid the way you were raised. Regardless of your own experience, it's important to be aware of what has shaped you and your approach to parenting. What do you want to change

from your childhood? Keep from your childhood? What do you want to show your children and give to them that you either had or did not have? Reflecting on and knowing your full self, embracing your strengths, and accepting your vulnerabilities can be challenging, but it's necessary so that you can see your child for who they are, unclouded by your past.

16. **Nuance matters**: My final tip seems like an obvious one but is one that still needs to be highlighted. Every child is different; every child is unique. What works for one at a given time may not apply well to another. Children have similar basic needs for security and sensitive, tuned-in care so that they can build trust in their primary caregiver. Yet each child develops inner safety and trust in their own individualized way. No single piece of advice can apply in the same way to every child. So remember that you know your child best. And when you are in connection with them, you will find ways to apply guidance and advice that work for you and for your child. Because tomorrow is a new day, and change will happen. You've got this.

Notes

CHAPTER 1: The Opportunity During Times of Uncertainty

12   Our reactions and the way our brains respond: Sonja K. Soo, Zenith D. Rudich, Bokang Ko, Alibek Moldakozhayev, Abdelrahman Alokda, and Jeremy M. Van Raamsdonk, "Biological resilience and aging: Activation of stress response pathways contributes to lifespan extension," *Ageing Research Reviews* 88 (2023): 101941.

12   This ability to adapt: Bryan Kolb and Robbin Gibb, "Brain plasticity and behaviour in the developing brain," *Journal of the Canadian Academy of Child and Adolescent Psychiatry* 20, no. 4 (2011): 265–76.

14   First, we become aware: Richard S. Lazarus and Susan Folkman, *Stress, Appraisal, and Coping* (New York: Springer, 1984).

16   If we can support: Richard J. Davidson and Bruce S. McEwen, "Social influences on neuroplasticity: Stress and interventions to promote well-being," *Nature Neuroscience* 15 (2012): 689–95.

17   Samuel Meisels: James W. Plunkett, Tovah Klein, and Samuel J. Meisels, "The relationship of infant-mother attachment to stranger sociability at three years," *Infant Behavior and Development* 11, no. 1 (1988): 83–96.

19   We titled this project: Judith S. Schteingart, Janice Molnar, Tovah P. Klein, Cynthia B. Lowe, and Annelie E. Hartmann, "Homelessness and child functioning in the context of risk and protective factors moderating child outcomes," *Journal of Clinical Child Psychology* 24, no. 3 (1995): 320–31; Janice M. Molnar, William R. Rath, and Tovah P. Klein, "Constantly compromised: The impact of homelessness on children," *Journal of Social Issues* 46, no. 4 (1990): 109–24.

22   The seminal work of: Myron A. Hofer, "The psychobiology of early attachment," *Clinical Neuroscience Research* 4, no. 5–6 (May 2005): 291–300, DOI:10.1016/j.cnr.2005.03.007.

23   At the same time: Martha F. Erickson, L. Alan Sroufe, and Byron Egeland, "The relationship between quality of attachment and behavior

problems in preschool in a high-risk sample," *Monographs of the Society for Research in Child Development* 50, no. 1/2 (1985): 147–66.

23   Researchers followed the Romanian orphans: Charles A. Nelson, Nathan A. Fox, and Charles H. Zeanah, *Romania's Abandoned Children: Deprivation, Brain Development, and Struggle for Recovery* (Cambridge, MA: Harvard University Press, 2014).

24   The more responsive the caregiver: Frances M. Lobo and Erika Lunkenheimer, "Understanding the parent-child coregulation patterns shaping child self-regulation," *Developmental Psychology* 56, no. 6 (June 2020): 1121–34.

25   More than a dozen: Klaus E. Grossman, Karin Grossman, and Everett Waters, *Attachment from Infancy to Adulthood: The Major Longitudinal Studies* (New York: Guilford Press, 2005).

25   Early in the study of attachment: Mary D. Salter Ainsworth, Mary C. Blehar, Everett Waters, and Sally N. Wall, *Patterns of Attachment: A Psychological Study of the Strange Situation* (New York: Lawrence Erlbaum, 1978).

26   As a result, studies show: Patty X. Kuo, Ekjyot K. Saini, Elizabeth Tengelitsch, and Brenda L. Volling, "Is one secure attachment enough? Infant cortisol reactivity and the security of infant-mother and infant-father attachments at the end of the first year," *Attachment & Human Development* 21, no. 5 (Oct 2019): 426–44.

27   This network of relationships: Jude Cassidy and Phillip R. Shaver, *Handbook of Attachment: Theory, Research, and Clinical Applications* (New York: Guilford Press, 2016).

27   Jack Shonkoff calls the: Jack P. Shonkof and Andrew S. Garner, Committee on Psychosocial Aspects of Child and Family Health, Committee on Early Childhood, Adoption, and Dependent Care, and Section on Developmental and Behavioral Pediatrics, Benjamin S. Siegel, Mary I. Dobbins, Marian F. Earls, Andrew S. Garner, Laura McGuinn, John Pascoe, and David L. Wood, "The lifelong effects of early childhood adversity and toxic stress," *Pediatrics* 129, no. 1 (2012): e232–e246.

27   The hidden regulators: Nina Graf, Roseanna M. Zanca, Wei Song, Elizabeth Zeldin, Roshni Raj, and Regina M. Sullivan, "Neurobiology of parental regulation of the infant and its disruption by trauma within attachment," *Frontiers in Behavioral Neuroscience* 16 (April 2022): 806323, doi: 10.3389/fnbeh.2022.806323.

CHAPTER 2: The You Factor

43   James Gross, a psychology professor at Stanford: J. J. Gross and
O. P. John, "Individual differences in two emotion regulation processes:
Implications for affect, relationships, and well-being," *Journal of Personality
and Social Psychology* 85, no. 2 (2003): 348–62, https://doi.org/10.1037/0022
-3514.85.2.348; M. van't Wout, L. J. Chang, and A. G. Sanfey, "The
influence of emotion regulation on social interactive decision-making,"
Emotion 10, no. 6 (Dec. 2010): 815–21, doi: 10.1037/a0020069. PMID:
21171756; PMCID: PMC3057682.

43   Indeed, back in the 1950s: Donald W. Winnicott, "Transitional
objects and transitional phenomena: A study of the first not-me possession,"
International Journal of Psychoanalysis 34, no. 2 (1953): 89–97; Donald W.
Winnicott, *The Child, the Family, and the Outside World* (Boston: Addison-
Wesley, 1964).

PART II: The Five Pillars of Your Child's Resilience

51   As you move through the pillars: T. Berry Brazelton and Joshua D.
Sparrow, *Touchpoints: The Essential Reference: Your Child's Emotional and
Behavioral Development* (Boston: Addison-Wesley, 1992).

CHAPTER 3: The Safety Net

58   In another example: Tovah P. Klein, Ellen R. Devoe, Claudia Miranda-
Julian, and Keri Linas, "Young children's responses to September 11th: The
NYC experience," *Infant Mental Health Journal* 30, no. 1 (2009): 1–22.

63   Indeed, researchers have shown: Naja Ferjan Ramírez, Sarah
Roseberry Lytle, and Patricia K. Kuhl, "Parent coaching increases
conversational turns and advances infant language development,"
Psychological and Cognitive Sciences 117, no. 7 (February 2020): 3484–91;
Elise A. Piazza, Marius Cătălin Iordan, and Casey Lew-Williams, "Mothers
consistently alter their unique vocal fingerprints when communicating with
infants," *Current Biology* 27, no. 20 (October 2017): 3162–67.

63   As children mature: Lauren S. Baron and Yael Arbel, "Inner speech
and executive function in children with developmental language disorder:
Implications for assessment and intervention," *Perspectives of the ASHA
Special Interest Groups* 7, no. 6 (December 2022): 1645–59.

63   It may be difficult to imagine: Goran Šimić, Mladenka Tkalčić, Vana Vukić, Damir Mulc, Ena Španić, Marina Šagud, Francisco E. Olucha-Bordonau, Mario Vukšić, and Patrick R. Hof, "Understanding emotions: Origins and roles of the amygdala," *Biomolecules* 11, no. 6 (June 2021): 823.

CHAPTER 4: The Balance Principle

92   The prefrontal cortex: Nim Tottenham, "The brain's emotional development," *Cerebrum* (July 2017): 8–17.

99   The goal is to keep: Daniel J. Siegel and Tina Payne Bryson, *The Whole-Brain Child* (New York: Random House, 2012).

100   Rodent and mammal studies: Megan R. Gunnar and Karina M. Quevedo, "Early care experiences and HPA axis regulation in children: A mechanism for later trauma vulnerability," *Progress in Brain Research* 167 (2007): 137–149.

100   The parent helps the child: Nina Graf, Roseanna M. Zanca, Wei Song, Elizabeth Zeldin, Roshni Raj, and Regina M. Sullivan, "Neurobiology of parental regulation of the infant and its disruption by trauma within attachment," *Frontiers in Behavioral Neuroscience* 16 (April 2022): 806323; Maya Opendak, Elizabeth Gould, and Regina Sullivan, "Early life adversity during the infant sensitive period for attachment: Programming of behavioral neurobiology of threat processing and social behavior," *Developmental Cognitive Neuroscience* 25 (2017): 145–59, https://doi.org/10.1016/j.dcn.2017.02.002, https://www.sciencedirect.com/science/article/pii/S1878929316300718.

101   As researchers note: S. Lu, F. Wei, and G. Li, "The evolution of the concept of stress and the framework of the stress system," *Cell Stress* 5, no. 6 (April 26, 2021): 76–85. doi: 10.15698/cst2021.06.250. PMID: 34124582; PMCID:PMC8166217.

101   "Short" exposures to stress: R. M. Sullivan, "The neurobiology of attachment to nurturing and abusive caregivers," *Hastings Law Journal* 63, no. 6 (August 2012): 1553–70. PMID: 24049190; PMCID: PMC3774302.

CHAPTER 5: The Freedom Trail

112   A 2015 study out of Harvard: Ronald F. Ferguson, Sarah F. Phillips, Jacob F. S. Rowley, and Jocelyn W. Friedlander, *The Influence of Teaching*

Beyond Standardized Test Scores: Engagements, Mindsets and Agency (Cambridge, MA: Harvard University: The Achievement Gap Initiative, 2015).

115 A large body of research: Sofie Kuppens, Eva Ceulemans. "Parenting styles: A closer look at a well-known concept," *Journal of Child and Family Studies* 28, no. 1 (2019): 168–81. https://doi.org/10.1007/s10826-018-1242-x.

116 first described in groundbreaking: Ibid.

128 The renowned Swiss cognitive: Herbert P. Ginsburg and Sylvia Opper: *Piaget's Theory of Intellectual Development, 3rd Edition* (Pearson, 1987).

128 I saw this type of thinking: Tovah P. Klein, "Seeing the Child's World: The essence of Anji True Play that can be transported to worldwide locations," True Play Conference, Anji, China (May, 2019) www.anjiplay.com.

133 Mogel continues: Wendy Mogel, *The Blessing of a B Minus: Using Jewish Teachings to Raise Resilient Teenagers* (New York: Scribner, 2011), 97.

CHAPTER 6: The Power of Connection

145 It's enormously important that: R. Ames, "Help-seeking and achievement orientation: Perspectives from attribution theory," in *New Directions in Helping*, vol. 2, eds. B. DePaulo, A. Nadler, and J. D. Fisher (New York: Academic Press, 1983), 165–86.

146 Scientists distinguish these: Kathy T. Do, Ethan M. McCormick, and Eva H. Telzer, "The neural development of prosocial behavior from childhood to adolescence," *Social Cognitive and Affective Neuroscience* 14, no. 2 (February 2019): 129–39.

147 For instance, social neuroscientist Lieberman: Matthew D. Lieberman, *Social: Why Our Brains Are Wired to Connect* (New York: Crown Publishers, 2013).

148 Children move closer to: Diane Poulin-Dubois, "Theory of mind development: State of the science and future directions," *Progress in Brain Research* 254, ch. 7 (Elsevier: 2020), 141–66.

164 Work by Joe Allen: Joseph P. Allen, Rachel K. Narr, Jessica Kansky, and David E. Szwedo, "Adolescent peer relationship qualities as predictors of long-term romantic life satisfaction," *Child Development* 91, no. 1 (2020): 327–40; Joseph P. Allen, Maryfrances Porter, Christy McFarland, Kathleen Boykin McElhaney, and Penny Marsh, "The relation of attachment security to adolescents' paternal and peer relationships, depression, and externalizing behavior," *Child Development* 78, no. 4 (2007): 1222–39.

167   research found that parents: Ibid.

172   We hear about the alarming: Office of the Surgeon General, *Our Epidemic of Loneliness and Isolation: The U.S. Surgeon General's Advisory on the Healing Effects of Social Connection and Community* (Washington, DC: US Department of Health and Human Services, 2023).

CHAPTER 7: The Gift of Acceptance

177   When our children learn to love: D. W. Winnicott, *The Child, the Family, and the Outside World* (Addison-Wesley Publishers, 1964).

188   The science unequivocally supports: Lisa Matricciani, Catherine Paquet, Barbara Galland, Michelle Short, and Tim Olds, "Children's sleep and health: A metareview," *Sleep Medicine Reviews* 46 (2019), 136–50, https://doi.org/10.1016/j.smrv.2019.04.011.

193   It also helps build our: Marcia P. Jimenez, Nicole V. DeVille, Elise Elliott, Jessica E. Schiff, Grete E. Wilt, Jaime E. Hart, and Peter James, "Associations between nature exposure and health: A review of the evidence." *International Journal of Environmental Research and Public Health* 18, no. 9 (2021): 1–19, http://dx.doi.org/10.3390/ijerph18094790.

197   Research has shown that: Kristin Homan and Lisa Hosack, "Gratitude and the self: Amplifying the good within," *Journal of Human Behavior in the Social Environment* 29. no. 7 (2019): 1–13, https://doi.org/10.1080/10911359.2019.1630345.

197   The research and its results: Geyze Diniz, Ligia Korkes, Luca Schiliró Tristão, Rosangela Pelegrini, Patrícia Lacerda Bellodi, and Wanderley Marques Bernardo, "The effects of gratitude interventions: a systematic review and meta-analysis," *Einstein (São Paulo)* 21 (August 2023).

199   Equally important is that mindfulness: Shelley H. Carson and Ellen J. Langer, "Mindful practice for clinicians and patients," in *Handbook of Primary Care Psychology* (2004): 173–83. Oxford University Press.

199   In their extensive research: Ibid.

200   Psychology professor and director: Richard J. Davidson and Alfred W. Kazniak, "Conceptual and methodological issues in research on mindfulness and meditation," *American Psychologist* 70, no. 7 (October 2015): 581–92.

Index

Note: *Italicized* page numbers indicate illustrations.

About the Author

TOVAH P. KLEIN, PhD, is a psychology professor at Barnard College, Columbia University; the director of the Center for Toddler Development; and the author of *How Toddlers Thrive: What Parents Can Do Today for Children Ages 2–5 to Plant the Seeds of Lifelong Success.* In her roles as a researcher and professor, and in direct care with parents and children for over thirty years, Klein has helped to define what every child needs to thrive, regardless of their life situation. She works with programs worldwide that address the needs of children, and is highly sought after as a developmental expert on a range of timely topics and an advisor to children's media and organizations, including National Geographic Kids, Apple TV+, the Children's Museum of Manhattan, the Hunts Point Alliance for Children, Room to Grow, and Ubuntu Pathways South Africa. She lives in New York City with her family.

BILLIE FITZPATRICK, MA, EdM, is a writer, educator, and coauthor of numerous bestselling titles related to psychology, neuroscience, regenerative medicine, and sexuality.

Tips, Advice, and Resources for Parents and Professionals

For additional guidance and support on any parenting journey, find:

Articles
Resources
Videos
Podcasts
Community
Workshops
Speaking
...and more!

www.tovahklein.com